The Mother of Honey

Ana Maria Luisa

For my mother, who fought so many battles for me and with me.

Iracy

A native Brazilian name from the indigenous Tupi-Guarani tribe, derived from elements of Yira *meaning honey and* su *meaning mother –* Iracy mae do mel *– the mother of the honey*

The keeper of stories

England, March 2015

The film is about to start, the evening ahead is planned. *Twelve Years a Slave* for Bianca and me, then dinner with Paul and Jack, who has refused point-blank to join us: 'far too depressing'. But in an hour or so the four of us will be reunited. Bianca will insist on sharing vivid details of the film. They will all laugh at my disheveled face and red, swollen eyes. Jack will stop before the others: 'Are you alright now?' I will cheer up at the sheer delight of being with them. Deep down they know the reason why such films affect me so deeply. But when I'm with them, there's no place I'd rather be, there's nothing else I desire from this world.

'Turn your phone off, it's about to start,' I whisper.

'Mum, it's Beatriz messaging me, I think we should go.' The look on her face, her calm determination taking control, makes me follow her out of the cinema.

Another blockage. A narrowing of her arteries, a severe reduction of blood flow, has landed her in hospital again. This is the third time in the past five years that a stroke has taken away her independence, her vitality and that incredible zest for life.

'She will bounce back, she always does,' my internal dialogue starts fast and

5

furious, 'when will be the best time to go, when will I be most useful to her?' Decisions that I have agonised over many times before.

News arrives fast that she is soon to be released from hospital. Paul busies himself looking for the best deals and soon I am booked on a flight to São Paulo. In less than sixteen hours I will be by her side.

'Mum, just go and do not worry about us. I am not sure if you noticed – we have grown up. Keep me informed. If you need anything, anything at all, message me. I will be online night and day.' Bianca hugs me tightly and gets into her car, hurrying back to her life in London. I watch her go: the absolute master of her universe.

'Jack, are you going to be ok? Please be careful with drinking and marijuana.'

He bursts out laughing. I welcome, and try to hold on to, that laughter. For some reason, he cannot help laughing every time I mention the word marijuana, deliberately pronounced in perfect Spanish. He takes a serious tone and, in that empathetic way of being that is so naturally his, says: 'Go, Mum, I won't starve, and I won't become a drug dealer either. There is no time, you will soon be back. I will take care of Dad for you.'

If only she could see them now, she would throw me one of her knowing looks: 'It was all worth it in the end, Kirinha, I was absolutely certain then as I am now.'

I bear-hug Paul outside the departure gate. All the tears I try so hard to hold in come at once. An avalanche of pent-up tension engulfs me.

'Hey, you, go in – grab a hot drink, a paper, try and distract yourself a little. We will be fine and I will take good care of the kids.'

I am soon high up in the clouds, alone, missing all three of them. Already missing what I now call home, thinking of when we will be reunited again.

But it has always been like this with me and her. When it matters, 9,000 miles, the Atlantic Ocean, the different twists and turns our journeys have taken, cannot keep us apart.

When it truly matters, nothing or no one can stop us from crossing that ocean.

São Paulo, March 2015

I find her lying in her bed, in her bedroom in her house, a tube coming out of her nose: the only way she can be fed and watered. Her body is frail. Her dark hair with only a few specks of grey – even in her eighties – has gone white overnight. The brown skin that used to glow has gone grey. She opens her arms; I collapse next to her in the bed and hug her gently. Suddenly I am the mother and she, the baby.

It is as clear to me as the Brazilian blue sky outside that she will never be the same again. For the very first time I see fear in her eyes – not fear of the world outside, for she knows she can fight external demons, but fear of the ogres within her body that are beyond her control. No, she is never going to be the same again.

Never!

Never to laugh out loud at her own stupid jokes.

Never to scheme.

Never to break all the rules and burn the rule book.

Never to plot and manipulate her way in and out of a life that has denied her and her loved ones even the most basic of human rights.

Never to show me her love – *fuba* cake love.

Never to give me her pearls of ancient Tupi-Guarani wisdom.

It's the very first night and I'm lying on the bed next to her. She wakes up in lot of pain. I take her to the bathroom, both of us struggling as she has lost control of her legs.

'I am giving you all this trouble, taking you away from your family,' she whispers through the pain.

Her words cut through me like a knife.

So, she has to leave her home. The home she fought so hard to buy, to build, to make her own – the garden she earthed up with her tiny green fingers, the orchids she lovingly cultivated to adorn her veranda. Oh, if that veranda could talk! It would tell rich stories of her children, grandchildren, great-grandchildren, sisters, brothers, cousins, distant cousins, and neighbours that visited often. In the safety of her veranda, eating *fuba* cake, washed down with endless *cafezinhos*, they would unburden their secrets to her looking for a bit of her ancient wisdom, longing to be heard. That veranda, where not so long ago she sat with her books, her memories, her dreams and her schemes – her little piece of heaven on this wretched earth.

From her little piece of heaven into an ambulance, then a hospital, then another ambulance, then another hospital where we both stay for nearly a month, she in the hospital bed, heavily medicated, ugly tubes everywhere to keep her stable, I in the sofa bed next to her, the pain-in-the-ass daughter, ensuring that she gets the care she deserves.

Now, before she is due to be discharged, as there is nothing further the medical staff can do for her, the realisation that she can no longer return to her home hits my brothers and me. Another ambulance ride and we arrive at the Teodoro Campos Sao Paulo Clinic – TCSP.

How alien these surroundings are to her, with unfamiliar sounds, smells and faces. The faces of care-assistants and nurses busy with their endless chores. And the faces of those who live there, locked in, their bodies and minds no longer fit to inhabit the outside world.

And here we sit at her final destination. Side by side, engulfed by a cruel silence, among strangers, suffocating in the prison of our fears.

'So, they are bringing the corpses in now, are they?'

I hear the voice before I see the face of the old man sitting across the room. He had been a lawyer or something – top of his tree – before dementia took over his mind.

'*Mamae*, don't listen to him, he's got dementia, he doesn't know what he is saying.'

Whispering in my ear, struggling to speak.

'The dementia only allows him to say what he really feels, I know a wanker when I hear one. Now tell him this from me – I will see him out. His dementia riddled brain will finish him off before my heart gives up on me.'

Oh, how I wish we could all scream out our combined rage at the injustice of being human.

Now it is 6pm, time to go, time to leave her here … 'breathe,' I'm telling myself. I breathe. I'm trying to hold back the sobs, trying hard to leave with some dignity and strength, trying to show her that I too can be dignified and strong just like her. Trying hard not to punch that old wanker sitting in front of us.

'Hey lady, come over here, sit the little one next to me, I will look out for her, make sure she gets what she needs.'

I walk over and learn that Dona Rita, an Italian immigrant of sound mind, has been living at the clinic for several years. She is a stoic Catholic and one of the kindest souls I will be blessed to know.

Hugging Dona Rita, pouring all my gratitude into one tight hug, I'm sitting *Mamae* next to her, gently hugging her, afraid of breaking her bones or pulling that awful tube held together by tape right across her nose, spoiling that beautiful face I have always loved so much. Dona Rita takes her hand, stroking it gently. Glancing at Dona Rita, and my tiny mum sitting next to her, a memory of my Auntie Orminda and the banter we used to have, sitting around, eating *fuba* cake at my *mamae*'s veranda, comes rushing back to me.

'Well of course there are angels, Kirinha, they are everywhere.'

'But I have never seen one, Auntie.'

'That's because you haven't learnt to see them, or you haven't needed them yet.'

I'm walking out of the clinic, breathing in São Paulo's air. I love my home city. It is a monster of a modern-day metropolis in the tropics. With eyes wide-open twenty-four seven, it never sleeps. It houses the mega rich, the industrious working night and day for the mega rich, the poor labouring for the mega rich and the industrious, the gangs on the streets, the gangs inside government buildings and inside the corporations, the poets, the artists, the thinkers, the dreamers, the hope of its

11

children, the danger of its streets, the beauty of its parks, the tragedy, the chaos and the order. A place of exorbitant prosperity and intolerable poverty. A melting pot of different cultures and customs. São Paulo is, to me, as beautiful and as tragic as life itself. It is also where she escapes to, and takes refuge.

My mind is travelling back in time, reliving Iracy's life.

There are so many stories in my head about so many remarkable yet flawed dysfunctional people, drifting in and out of my awareness, that I can even hear their voices from time to time. It is as if they have somehow travelled through some channel or dimension within the labyrinth of my psyche so that we can say the odd hello or share a memory or two. Yet these stories help me through the course of my existence: to make some sense of what shaped my early concepts, beliefs and way of being in the world. But we are not static creatures: we are, if we allow ourselves to be, ever changing, constantly being shaped by evolving interior factors as well as new external influences.

I have never given any thought, whatsoever, to what will happen to these stories once I am dead and gone; they are just stories of lives that lived long ago. Lives of significant others whose greatest gift to me was to make me feel loved and that I mattered in their lives. I have shaped my own life with this imperfect love that I have managed to rescue from all those influences, learnt behaviours and experiences. Now I am just another imperfect love-giver in my own right, walking arm in arm with new-found souls, trying to understand their hearts – these hearts I have been brave enough to allow into mine.

Until I was prompted to share, the stories that live inside my head were simply part of the tapestry of my family history. I wonder whether this new-found hunger for these stories by her grandchildren is linked to her dying. Her grandchildren have already experienced losses, some more than others, but to me the thought of her inevitable departure has created within my core an almost uncontrollable need to remember her colourful and courageous life. This mother whom I love, who fought so many battles for me and with me is far too significant to simply disappear. She is a world, a universe, a giver of life – the one who nurtured life, my life. How can I allow her to cease altogether? She gave me the gift of stories. Each one of us is a story to be told. When all is said and done, despite all the beliefs we hold about the world and about ourselves, it is the stories that remain to comfort us, to help us grow, to help us try and make some sense of our fleeting existences.

Time is a strange man-made concept based on our mortality and, in the greater scheme of things, our existences are very short indeed. There are no inherent measures of time. Time just rolls on and on, never ceasing.

Not even in her wildest dreams could my mother have imagined how her children, grandchildren and great-grandchildren would live only a few decades away. Nor can I imagine how my own children and their families will live when I am no longer around to share stories.

So here I am, the keeper of all the stories she told me, the stories I witnessed myself and the stories that I am not sure I should share at all. I am uncertain of how I can even begin to do justice to this tiny indigenous woman who would go around with flip-flops held together by bits of string so that I could have shiny shoes. How can I help her grandchildren grasp the kind wisdom of her soul, her unbreakable spirit? This amazing survivor who would pretend not to be hungry so there was more to go around for her children, who took in her nephews and nieces when they arrived unannounced, running away from their parents, from the street gangs, from the police.

But I have made a start and will continue and see what comes out of it. Maybe I will get a little help along the way from those whispering voices or from my dreams or from the dimensions within the labyrinth of my psyche. I feel that I have a Herculean task – to capture the fleeting past and stake a claim to it in the present.

This I will do for you my children, nephews and nieces and your children, for those who lived before her, with her and for those who will continue to live long after she is gone. And live we must. If possible, with some of her delicious, triumphant and courageous zest!

And if you wish you can continue to tell the story from your own unique insights, perspectives and experiences. You will, for sure, have a reader in me.

Jingle bells jingle all the way

The house is ready, the food kind of prepared or in the process of preparing itself as it often does in 21st century England. I can only imagine what my mother and grandmother went through preparing meals from scratch to an army of hungry children and extended families on such an insanely small budget. Just thinking about their plight exhausts me, saddens me, makes me think of them as superwomen. My mother had the great skill of feeding a hungry family of six with one chicken – but wait – not just for one day, but an entire week. The chicken casserole would transform itself, as if by magic, into a chicken risotto then a thick chicken soup and find its way into many pasta and couscous dishes. The multiplying chicken was one hundred per cent free-range: I plucked its feathers myself. The vegetables most likely organic! Had she been, like my aunties, a devoted member of the Assembly of God, I would swear divine intervention had something to do with this miraculously transforming chicken.

I loved all the creative dishes that came out of one single chicken. What I could not stomach was having to eat, day after day, the remains of a 'feijoada,' the Brazilian national

16

dish. Traditionally, the slaves cooked the food for the *senhoras* using the sought-after cuts of pork. The remains of the pig such as the ears, tails, tongue, snout, trotters and head were thrown away. The slaves rescued the pig's unwanted remains from the garbage and transformed them into a hearty, aromatic stew, packed with seasoning and padded out with black beans. It was the perfect meal to sustain the servants who sweated all day in the tropical heat, and helped to fend off colds and ailments during the colder winter months.

Iracy made the *feijoada* the traditional way: every bit of the unwanted pig went into the casserole. My brothers and I still laugh at an interminable *feijoada* that finally ended with my brother Heathcliff screaming when he found the eye of the pig staring at him from the plate. We all screamed in shock and disgust.

She was a miracle worker feeding us all with such creativity!

Of course, I am looking at her plight from my own perspective living in a Western society where around 15 million tonnes of food are thrown way every year, with almost fifty per cent coming from our homes. When I stop and try to see it her way, she felt blessed to be able to feed her family the best way she could: so far none of her children had died of starvation.

She grew up in rural Minas Gerais in Brazil, a daughter of farm labourers: just a fancy name to camouflage the fact that slavery still went on, with wealthy farmers paying such appalling wages to their workers that it left their families dying of starvation and related diseases. Once she told me, in her matter-of-fact tone, how she would drink water until her belly felt full.

Drinking dirty water to keep hunger at bay

Dancing in the moonlight until the break of day.

'At my brief time at school, Kirinha, as soon as the bell went, I used to run out of the classroom to the taps outside and fill my belly with water. It really helped to stop those embarrassing noises coming out of my middle.'

As I observe the interaction of my nephews and my own children, I am filled with nothing but pride combined with a certain relief. They have escaped their family's history of alcoholism and poor mental health. A Christmas Eve free from drunken fights, and hurtful abusive words followed by the deep shame and that crucifying sorrowfulness so common in families impacted by alcoholism. Here, a cycle has been broken.

Douglas, my young brother's first born, his wife Ligia and their three-year-old son, Leo, have just arrived from São Paulo to spend Christmas with us and visit parts of Europe. Vinicius, my oldest brother's son, and his wife Magga – who is pregnant with her first child – are also here. They live in England. These nephews of mine are young professionals living their lives in much better surroundings with so many more opportunities.

'Auntie, I am surprised that you have finally learnt how to throw a few dishes together,' said Douglas, mocking me.

'You will find that the assistant chef does a lot of the planning in this kitchen,' Vinicius joins in, already laughing.

'Naaa,' says Jack, 'it is all pre-prepared. All she will do is move the items on her Christmas menu from this white icebox straight into the oven.'

'Jack, shush!! Our honoured guests have travelled far and wide just to enjoy my cooking.'

Bianca walks in and opens the freezer.

'What is this, *Mamae*? A beef Wellington!?!'

They fall about, laughing hysterically now. Their Brazilian cousins have never heard of beef Wellington.

Little Leo runs in dressed as Spider-Man, throws a massive imaginary web on top of us all, squats on the floor spreading his little hands and spider fingers in perfect Spider-Man style and shouts.

'BOOM! Got all of you suckers with one massive web, THWIP.'

Paul comes in and finally puts some order to the commotion.

'Now all of you, get out! Or start showing off your culinary skills.'

And off they go. I'm watching each one of them: strong, capable, joyous and balanced individuals. She would be so proud to see the happy, healthy faces of her grandchildren and her little great-grandson all gathered in my kitchen, in this 100-year old house: my home, reformed, extended, decorated with soft tones, with an idyllic garden with a little bridge over a pond and hundreds of different species of flowers, shrubs, young fruit trees, ancient trees; created by Paul's labour of love – our arduous love over the years. On occasions like these I often become very aware that if it wasn't for her courage, her sharp intuition, her selfless love for me and her total belief in me, my life might have been very different now.

I wonder what she would think if she saw her granddaughters-in-law, in deep conversation about the high and lows of being working mothers, the pluses and minuses of living in Brazil or England, and the state of worldwide educational systems. They are strong, independent women. She would be proud of how her grandsons treat their wives and the harmonious equality of their relationships.

'Time and the courage of some, Kirinha, changes everything, even if takes a few decades. What we cannot do is stop moving forward little by little,' I am certain she would have said it just like that.

The Christmas lunch is going well apart from the beef Wellington, which remains slightly frozen despite the instructions on the box being followed with precision. My beef Wellington is the in-joke this Christmas among my Brazilian guests, my Anglo-Brazilian children and my one hundred per cent English husband.

I think of her in her care home, a victim of another cruel stroke that has left her unable to care for herself, a stroke that took not only her independence away but that vibrant light that shone from her. Yet I don't feel sadness, just acceptance and a gladness knowing that, despite it all, the fruits of her tree continue to blossom through a new generation of evolved young people in ways that surprise me every day.

The stories she shared with me, the things I witnessed, in time, give me the tools to try to understand. Trying to understand serves me well to this day. The more I understand the less I fear, the less I hurt. This creates inner space to love more deeply, to laugh more loudly and to accept my own flawed humanity.

A Broken Fairy Tale

Here romance did not die; it was just never given the chance to be born.

Serrania, Minas Gerais around 1920

It was one of those baking hot Sundays. The heat coming from the dirt track road burnt the soles of his scruffy black shoes. The blazing sun beating down on his head, shoulders and neck made him wish that he could escape the heat by jumping into the first river or lake along the way. His lopsided hat was stuck to his head by the sheer intensity of his perspiration, caused not only by the heat of the day but also by the anxiety he was beginning to feel. It was a big step Joao Inacio da Silva had decided to take. He had been in Minas Gerais for quite a while now. He liked the long days working in the fields. He had learnt the ropes quickly, got on well with the boss and with his co-workers. He was making a small living and kept himself out of trouble. But it was the long, dark evenings and nights that had begun to unsettle him. He was already twenty-six years of age and unmarried. Loneliness was knocking at his door. What started with a faint knock, easily ignored, was now an insistent almost angry loud knock that kept him awake at night.

He had been walking for a few hours and there was still no sign of the house. He

22

muttered to himself as he stopped, sitting down under a tree to cool himself down.

'What if the lads are having me on? What if there is no such family living at the end of this dirt road?'

So far, he had only stumbled upon a few farms with the common small dwellings built for farm labourers. He was tired, his temper, which always got the better of him, was beginning to rise in his chest. Full of doubts, putting his sweaty hat back on, he carried on. However, the break under the shady tree and the idyllic prettiness of the region with its green fields that stretched for miles and miles, its magnificent ancient trees populated by colonies of colourful birds with their constant soothing song, had cooled him and his temper down.

At that time Serrania was a small town in Minas Gerais. Situated by the crystal-clear waters of the river Ribeiro São Tome, migrants would settle there to work on the coffee plantations. Everything was so recent in that part of the world that so many things lacked names and so one had to rely on people's memories and interpretations of what they saw or heard.

He knew little about the family he was going to visit. He had heard they lived at the end of the road he had been walking on since the early hours. There was never any mention of the man of the house. The mother of the daughters he was hoping to meet had a bit of a reputation. She was indigenous, a true Tupi-

Guarani; her life had been shrouded by rumours. It was thought that she was given a house by a rich farmer who had taken her as his mistress and fathered her last two children – Francisca and Pedro. And all of this was orchestrated by the farmer's wife who had fallen ill and travelled back to Europe searching for a cure. According to some, the farmer's wife had left her husband and young children in very capable hands.

Joao Inacio walked on, lost in thought. He was thirsty and could hear the gruesome noises coming from his empty belly. He cut a lonesome figure in his tight, worn-out suit, drenched in sweat. The look on his face did not betray the anxiety he felt, usually manifested by a tight pain in his chest and the fear that he would stutter and make a fool of himself. The gift of the gab had eluded him, so he preferred to say as little as possible. He was nervous in social situations, especially in front of young women.

An hour or so later he spotted the house. It was a good-sized house with white walls that had turned a dirty shade of grey. The window shutters had seen better days and hung off their hinges. But there was no doubt in his mind that this was the house; his workmate's description of it was spot on. The chickens in the front yard pecked lazily at the few grains of corn thrown on the ground. A couple of old dogs tried to sleep as a swarm of flies wreaked havoc in their scabby fur. He stood there contemplating turning right back and starting the long walk back to his digs when the door opened. The lady of the house greeted him.

'And how can I help you, Sir?' Years of serving Europeans and their descendants had taught her how to greet a white man, even if the one standing in front of her was so much worse off than herself.

'Mm— ma— my nn— naa— mme is Joao Inacio da Silva,' he stuttered, taking his hat off in a pathetic attempt to greet her and introduce himself.

'Yes, we have heard about you, and we were beginning to worry that you got lost along the way or got eaten by flies in this heat.' She laughed a loud carefree laugh, 'Come on in and meet my girls.'

He was struck by how clean, cool and impeccably tidy the house looked inside. The living area, though small, had comfortable chairs upholstered in tasteful patterns that matched the curtains. The stone floor was cool and so clean you could eat your dinner from it. There was a small sideboard filled with homemade goods made from maize – typical Tupi-Guarani dishes.

She gestured him to sit down. She called her girls who came in looking excited and puzzled.

'Well, I will leave you youngsters to get to know each other and go and fetch some cool lemonade.'

With the mother gone, a cruel silence engulfed him and the young ladies standing in front of him. After what seemed like an eternity, he noticed their complicity as they rudely looked him up and down, whispering in each other's ears, trying hard not to laugh. He felt his face burn, his throat began to choke. He was saved by the return of the mother followed by a very young girl carrying a tray with a jar of lemonade. The young girl looked at him, and he noticed a concerned look on her face. She looked at her giggling sisters, threw them an evil look, turned to him and poured him a glass of lemonade. He gulped it down letting a loud burp fill the room. They all fell about laughing: he wished the ground would open and swallow him alive or that he would be struck by a fatal heart attack right there and then!

'It is ok, here have another glass, you have been walking under this blazing sun all morning.'

At that moment he not only saw the young girl in front of him, with her long, shiny, black plaits, white pinafore dress, beautiful dark skin and the sweetest smile he had ever seen, he also saw the character of a young girl wise beyond her years. He felt her kindness and her concern for him.

During the following hours the girls busied themselves serving the stranger. The food they had prepared in the morning was a feast never experienced before by Joao. He attacked the food with gusto; his table manners left a lot to be desired. But they all tried to make him feel at home. As he relaxed he could ask a few questions and answer the mother's questions about his work and how he was finding that part of the world. Everyone noticed that as hard as he tried he could not take his eyes off young Francisca.

The words Joao Inacio da Silva uttered as he got up to leave would change the course of young Francisca's life forever.

'I want to take young Francisca, Ma'am.'

They all stopped to look at him, trying to take in what he had just said.

'Well, though she is already able to bear a child, she is only thirteen years old!'

Francisca looked at him with a mixture of horror and a young girl's pride for being chosen. She blushed, hiding behind her mother.

'Francisca is only a child, Joao Inacio, she is not even handy around the house. She spends her time making dolls from sweetcorn cobs for the kids around here.'

He was having none of it and without much of a fight for her young daughter she agreed that he could take her. There was never any mention of a courtship, engagement or even a proper wedding.

Francisca, although scared at what life had just thrown at her, felt a certain amount of affection for Joao's helplessness. The same kind of affection and concern she felt for the stray kids, dogs and cats she was always trying to rescue. She was kind to a fault – a kindness she would bestow upon me so many times when I was growing up. She did what she saw her mother do all her life and accepted her fate, trying to make the best of a situation she had no control over.

Joao accomplished the task he set out to do on that baking hot Sunday and claimed the companion that would stop loneliness from knocking at his door at night. But he soon brought her back to her mother. He was angry and tired of finding her making tiny rag dolls or playing a game of tag with kids in the neighbourhood when he came home from working in the fields.

'Ma'am she does not know how to run a house, everything she tries to cook is a disaster, wh— wh— what if she sets the place on fire, what if I am not there and she goes up in flames?'

Francisca's mother could see and feel his distress, but she also noticed his concern for her youngest. But above all, she noticed the change in her daughter. She looked distant, her eyes that used to shine with excitement at the slightest little things looked dull and a touch troubled.

As a young girl, Francisca sometimes thought, and even dreamt, of getting married and having a family. But the ordeal that began with her first night with Joao Inacio, immersed her in a hopeless cycle where she was impoverished and plagued with health problems. A wretched legacy to pass on to her future daughters.

'Don't worry, let me keep her here with me during the day for a while and I can assure you she will get the training she needs to be a wife.'

'Ummm,' he hesitated at the thought of being without her, 'bring her back each evening.'

Those days spent close to her mother, who patiently taught her how to cook without waste (a skill she would pass on to her own daughters), how to sew, how to do the laundry, and how to appease her husband's temper, were very precious to young Francisca. It meant that no matter what was happening to her, what fear and confusion she felt, she had her mother and her sisters. She realised that she could visit. That they could still be part of her life. This kept her going. Without too many words, her mother taught her that she was not all powerless in her union with Joao and that her husband needed her and already seemed lost at the thought of not having her there.

'You are too young to understand, Francisca. Only time and your own experiences will make you wise so that you can pass on your wisdom to your children. You will see that it is not the most intelligent, or the strongest and not even the most beautiful that survive but the most adaptable. You are a Tupi-Guarani like me. Your ancestors before you lived in harmony with this land, women

29

were respected, worshipped even, for having the gift of giving life. Now we are ruled by men and women who are blind, hungry for gold and sick in the heart.'

Francisca listened quietly, enjoying her mother's soothing voice, her warmth, her love, thinking, trying to make sense of those words. She tried to imagine what her mother had to go through to adapt and survive.

Francisca had always been her mother's pet. Her mother had always felt a desperate love for her youngest, who was born with a fragile constitution, respiratory problems and a wondering mind. She always seemed lost in her own world of angels, spirits and fairies. Her mother never knew where her faith had originated from. She was a true believer in life after death and seemed to care little for this world. She was blessed with a sharp intuition and trust, which she used to navigate her life.

On that baking hot Sunday when Joao Inacio came to claim Francisca, her mother had no hesitation consenting to their union. Although her daughter was still a child, she felt a responsibility to ensure the survival of her daughters; in Joao Inacio she saw an opportunity not to be missed. She felt it would be difficult to find someone to take on such a fragile girl always wheezing and lost in thought.

My great-grandmother, whose Tupi name is unknown, had to make baffling choices. These choices could be perceived to an outsider as hard-heartened, inhuman even. But such choices violated the core of my great-grandmother's being. They wiped out her origins, her ancestry and took away her hope. Handing over her youngest and most frail daughter to that stranger left her bereaved. But what choice did she have? Until she took her last breath, even when she went completely blind, she was there for Francisca, guiding her on the sidelines. Thus, Francisca had to stop playing with her rag dolls. From that day on, overnight, she was forced to grow up. By day her mother trained her in all the domestic tasks required by a wife of a farm labourer in the 1920s in rural Brazil. Early evening, in time to prepare his meal, she returned to her husband; thirteen-year-old Francisca became a child bride in a corner of the world where everything was so recent that so many things lacked names.

> *No flowers*
> *No Valentine*
> *No girly romantic dreams*
> *Of a prince charming walking by*

But her mother's intuition was right. Joao Inacio and Francisca's union lasted over fifty years. Life had many surprises in store for them both. While his temper grew worse, Francisca's wisdom and benevolence grew stronger. She was the only one who could reason with him, calm him down and reprimand him when he went too far. Her presence was, to him, as vital as the air he breathed.

I know hardly anything about Joao Inacio da Silva, my grandfather the child snatcher. I know nothing of his family, but he appeared to be of European descent. I remember being told that he became very ill when he went to São Paulo and was working in appalling conditions in the construction industries sprawling in various parts of the fast-growing city.

I heard stories of his anger and cruelty. He used to beat up his sons and grandsons with a heavy stick, until they were left bleeding and almost unconscious on the floor. As I don't know his story, I find it difficult to understand. I heard he beat them up to make them grow up decent God-fearing men. I feel his brutal and powerless existence meant that he had to exercise his male dominance somehow. But what do I know? Without a safe harbour or a place to call home, some of his flesh and blood ran into the streets of São Paulo, soon becoming petty criminals and then developing the skills to join drug gangs. Some ended up in prison, some dead and one of them, after servicing his sentence, somehow made it to the top of his profession. He is now a jolly man with his own family and a successful business. Decades later this cousin of mine would rescue his surviving brothers and sisters who were trying to make a living in any way they could on the streets of São Paulo.

My grandparents went on to have sixteen children but sadly seven died while still very young through malnutrition and other related diseases. Despite the brutal circumstances of her life and her many losses, my grandmother – *vovó Chiquinha* – grew in benevolence and wisdom; from her, I learnt not only the importance but the healing benefits of kindness. She was the keeper of our young heart's secrets and our protector. She was famous for making a huge omelette with just a couple of eggs and bicarbonate of soda. It was a very impressive omelette until you cut it and it evaporated into nothing. But it made us laugh a great deal and we called it 'Grandma's wind omelette'.

The last memory I have of her was when my mum woke up in the middle of the night in a panic saying that grandma was calling her. We lived miles away with no telephone or car. Somehow, my father managed to appear with a jeep out of nowhere in the middle of the night. When we got there she was dying. Still in her sixties, she looked decades older. She had a hunchback due to a fall that was never attended to. Sixteen pregnancies and the unimaginable pain of burying so many of her young children had finally taken its toll on her frail body and she died in my mother's arms. My mother was the last of her children to get there to say her goodbyes. Maybe there is such a thing as telepathy after all. Maybe we are truly connected by love. I remember her funeral, the coffin opened in the lounge of her humble home, dozens or maybe over a hundred people coming to pay their respects. My mum did not shed a single tear. She never cried. She could not cry.

Reviews of empirical, clinical, and theoretical resources on trauma and trauma therapies suggest that dissociative experiences frequently follow traumatic experience. Only now are we beginning to gather sufficient data to understand the impact trauma, such as the ones experienced by my mother and her siblings, can have on an individual. I believe that by the age of seven she had already experienced so much trauma and loss that her defence mechanisms were firmly in place. Just as well. I feel if she had allowed herself to cry she may never have stopped. Maria, her older sister, however, cried a lot and her defence mechanisms appeared weak in comparison, this may explain why her life took such disastrous turns.

Hide and seek, peek a boo babies, where are you?

Serrania, Minas Gerais around 1934

There are certain stories that play over in my mind now and again. I remember them today just as vividly as when they were first shared with me. I never want to forget them for I have learnt to embrace them with as much courage and grace as I can master. They help me to understand so much about the people who brought me into this world. Reliving these stories makes me feel as if I am entering the lives of those farm labourers who became city dwellers and migrants to escape starvation and in doing so gave me a much better chance of survival. Their courage meant that my life was not as brutal.

Francisca, my grandmother, was constantly trying to recover from the many ailments and more serious diseases that went hand in hand with being pregnant and giving birth before her body had a chance to fully develop. In the early 1930s the mortality rate in that part of Brazil was high. The mortality rate in my grandparents' household was just as high. Each loss of a baby or young child left a cavernous vacancy in Francisca's heart, leaving her bereaved and empty. It was the emptiness that would never heal.

Francisca lost a lot of blood during the long hours of a difficult birth. When baby Iracy finally arrived, Francisca was too weak to hold or nurse her.

When hearing that my grandmother was unable to breastfeed her new-born, a rich farmer's wife sent the family a cow. Iracy, my mother, did not enjoy maternal closeness, nurture or breast milk, which are so vital to the first few weeks of a baby's life. She was raised by her eldest sister, Maria, on fresh cow's milk.

It was a reoccurring joke between my mother and her sisters how she used to crawl to her cow and sit there whimpering to be fed. They laughed, tears of laugher running down their sunburnt cheeks, 'Ha, Ha. Iracy's mother was a cow. Ha …' laughing away too much sorrow.

But Maria could never laugh her sorrow way like the others and her laugh would soon change into tears.

Maria was only eight years of age when she became a carer for her baby sister. The alliance between these two sisters, and how they helped each other throughout their lives, never ceased to surprise and inspire me. I am yet to witness a love so strong.

The diversity of uses and meanings combined with the complexity of the feelings involved makes love unusually difficult to define. However, the bond that existed between these two sisters, to me it will always represent the beauty and force of human kindness, compassion and affection. Their unselfish, loyal and benevolent concern for the good of the other will stay with me forever. It was a rare gift their shared.

Iracy must have been no more than seven years old when one of her younger sisters, who had been playing with her in the yard just a couple of days before, became ill. She had a fever and a rash all over her body, however, there was no medical centre for miles. A *curandeira* (healer) was called and arrived with a bunch of herbs and potions. After the second night it was obvious that the child was not getting any better. In desperation, Francisca picked up her sick little girl and left the house, walking towards the medical centre in the hope that a kind soul would offer her a lift along the way. My mother shared her vivid memories with me; she was playing outside without a care in the world when she heard her mother's screams. She told me that she would never forget how surreal this whole episode was and the feeling of helpless panic upon hearing her mother scream like a wounded animal; those screams that told a thousand stories of rage of injustice, of degradation of the human spirit. She was certain that those screams could be heard by her proud ancestors who once lived dignified existences on that very same hot terracotta soil, under that very same clear blue sky and blazing sun. She looked at her mother, carrying her little sister, from a distance but all she could see was a motionless pair of legs dangling like a rag doll.

I asked my mother how she felt that day, what went on in her head, in her mind, in her heart and she replied, 'I remember feeling panic and fear but then I felt nothing, just a bit annoyed that I would not have anyone to play with,' she went on, 'it had happened before, children were always dying and being buried all around Serrania's fields, it was just the way it was, and I used to play on their graves.

Hide and seek
Peek a boo
Babies, babies where are you
Ring a ring of roses
A pocket full of posies
A-Tishoo A-Tishoo
We all fall down.'

and she laughed … laughed way too *much sorrow.*

My aunties would always remind me that when one door shuts God always opens another. Soon after her little sister's death, a teacher came to visit the house. The teacher was called Roseli and she proudly announced that a school would be opening soon in the next village. By then my mum's mind was full of questions, ready and eager to learn. After pleading with her mum and dad, they allowed her to walk miles to the school, barefoot under the smouldering heat. She loved the teacher and the kids. She came back full of energy and

38

stories to tell. The teacher came back to the house just a few months later.

'She is very bright, very eager to learn. I am impressed at how fast she is progressing. She is very popular with the kids, even the children of the farmers have taken to her.'

Life was going well, Iracy was feeling alive and excited. Roseli's praise filled her with a strong desire to learn, to do well, to make her young teacher smile.

But after a year or so that brand-new door slammed shut in her face. One of the children, the daughter of one of the wealthiest farmers around Serrania, took a dislike to Iracy. The teachers knew the dislike was out of pure jealousy. Iracy's intelligence and hunger for knowledge combined with her maturity made her instantly popular with the teachers and the kids alike.

The farmer's daughter grew insanely jealous. The parents soon found out who was the cause of their precious princess's unhappiness. In no time, they ensured Iracy was sent home without a word of explanation and told never to return!

That afternoon, instead of skipping back home with her new-found enthusiasm, eager to share everything with her mum and siblings, she walked with a heavy heart, full of confusion and guilt, trying to understand what she had done wrong.

She walked slowly, listening to the birds, humming the songs she had learnt at school.

She was learning fast that the biggest lessons were not taught at school.

Francisca could not grasp why her daughter was so distraught: 'Well never mind, you have learnt a lot. Anyway, you couldn't have stayed on, we need you to work. Your dad is already asking round to get you a job either in the fields or doing domestic work.'

Early the next morning Roseli appeared at the house, she wanted to clarify a few things.

Iracy was so pleased to see her teacher again. To her she was just magnificent. A human/teacher/angel hybrid. She loved the way she spoke, so clearly, so softly, in a slow sing-song kind of way, using such beautiful words, always fixing her eyes on you to hold your attention. She loved even more the way she listened, taking her time, eyes fixed on you trying her very best to understand beyond the words, trying to listen with her heart – such a big heart.

'*Senhora* Francisca, I am dropping by to tell you that Iracy did nothing wrong, it is just that,' – she paused for a few seconds trying to use the words she had rehearsed that morning – 'the scheme I tried to introduce by giving the children of the labourers the chance to attend school has been scrapped by the farmers.' She paused again looking at the ground, 'You know they finance the local school, there was nothing I could do.'

Francisca took her hands, 'Well it is so kind of you to come all the way here and explain this to me. We would need an army of teachers like you to teach kids like my daughter. Go in peace, you have done all you can.'

She turned to Iracy. 'I got you some more books and some fun magazines, don't stop reading Iracy and don't ever forget how smart, funny and kind you are.'

Iracy picked up her things. 'I am going to work to help my parents, am not like the other girls, am I?'

'No, you are not. Your life is very different from theirs, Iracy. You will be a working girl now, just like me. The girls at school are still very immature, they are like babies and you are having to grow up fast!'

Iracy's heart filled with pride. She was only ten years old but felt ten feet tall! She threw her little arms around her teacher, hugging her for the last time.

Roseli walked away trying hard not to howl out the anger she felt inside.

She learned the hard lesson that her hands were too small to hold all the pain in the world. She learned that she was too weak and alone to teach the children that deserved a place in her classroom. She learned that to make a difference in this world was going to break her heart again and again.

Iracy soon bounced back. Joao found her domestic work at a farmer's house. She was proud to be working, and had a little time to read the books left around the house. On payday, she used to run home and proudly give her mum her wages.

Carl Rogers, one of the founders of humanistic psychology, believed that humans have one basic motive, that is the tendency to self-actualise – i.e. to fulfil one's potential and achieve the highest level of 'human-beingness' we can. What I always found most remarkable about my mum is how strongly this force Rogers called self-actualisation existed within her.

In most cases, such dreadful circumstances would mean that she could easily have followed her mother's plight or develop poor mental health. However, at the age of thirteen, instead of becoming yet another child bride, she decided to join her sister Maria who had moved to São Paulo. She was hoping for better paid work.

Although Maria could not write, Iracy regularly received beautifully-written letters that everyone was certain were written by Maria's boyfriend. She loved those letters. She started dreaming of São Paulo: the street fairs, the trams, the colours, the people and the great jobs with proper city wages.

The events that followed her arrival in the great capital of São Paulo would shape the entire fate of her parents and surviving siblings, as well as her future family.

A journey of a thousand miles begins from beneath one's feet
Lao Tzu

São Paulo, 1940

From beneath her tiny, rough, rural feet, her life journey begins.

To her mother and father, going to São Paulo was an alien concept. They had never left the fields of Serrania. The harshness of their daily existence, the losses of so many children combined with malnutrition, not to mention undiagnosed ailments, brutalised Joao Inacio and Francisca to such an extent that they failed to comprehend anything beyond their quest for survival.

Iracy's announcement was greeted with indifference, the kind that hides fear. Maria had already gone: to lose another daughter was something they could not face. Much easier to pretend it was not happening, much easier to ignore her announcement and hope Iracy would forget about the crazy idea.

But the lack of interest did not faze her. Nothing or no one would make her deviate from her plan. She was the master of all plans.

She was obsessed. I have seen her in this state of sheer obsession many times, at life-changing times like this; her intuition was so strong that it made her invincible.

In time, she managed to get a one-way ticket to São Paulo. When she told the lady she worked for, she was treated not only with indifference but annoyance at the inconvenience.

'So many of you now think that the answers to all your prayers are in São Paulo. What will most certainly happen is that you will end up working just as hard and end up in the slums sprawling around the city. Or, for a young girl like you, worse, much worse. That place is being flooded and destroyed by stupid migrants.'

Iracy said nothing.

'Well, if you have made up your mind then ask your mother to send one of your sisters to replace you. And by the way, you cannot travel with these worn-out flip-flops, take this pair of shoes, I never liked them.'

'Would you like me to fetch your sweet water, Ma'am.'

'Go, go, fetch me my water before you go and don't forget to talk to your mother about your replacement.'

Walking slowly to the kitchen, Iracy grabbed a tall glass, spit into it several times until the bottom of the glass was covered with a thick blob of her spit. She poured the sugar, added the water and gave it a stir. Walking slowly to the lounge she handed the lady the glass. Without saying another word, she walked out of that house holding the hand-me-down shoes, humming a little tune.

I remember how she was always humming a little tune or singing a nursery rhyme or a tune from the radio. She never showed her distress to the outside world. It was as if nothing bothered her much, as if she was untouched by her circumstances. The worse the crisis, the more she hummed, the louder she sang. Always humming and singing too much sorrow, too much anger away.

Even now, sitting in the care home, a shadow of her former self, with her once sharp mind drifting in and out of focus, her tiny body being carried like a bag of bones from bed to wheelchair from wheelchair to the sofa, all she needs is a prompt to burst into song with her now-strained croaky voice. But little do they know how deceiving her tiny frame and sweet exterior are. Only those who have tried to cross her have experienced her fury.

The last person to cross her and feel the full power of her scorn was an elderly woman at the clinic in São Paulo. This woman suffered with dementia and had a reputation for being plain evil, even before her mind was no longer any use for her deeds. She would call the nurses or helpers, and as soon as they got close enough, she would punch or scratch their faces, calling them all the filthy obscenities under the sun. Then one day at lunchtime, my mother, who was still walking at that time though with great difficulty, approached the sofa where this woman was sitting and immediately noticed her stick her legs out. She had the habit of doing this in order to trip whoever walked past her. Iracy calmly stopped, sat next to her and whispered.

'You don't fool me. Dementia or not you are an evil bitch. If you ever try to trip me again, I will fuck up your face so badly, you will end up looking even uglier than you already are. Don't fuck with me, is that clear?'

Dona Rita told me every detail of this interaction when I visited the following year, laughing, 'I am glad the little one is on my side.'

Francisca cried on the morning of Iracy's departure.

'Whose idea, was it? Maria, now you. I will never see either of you again. Lost in that sin city.'

'I will come and fetch you, Dad and the others, don't you worry.'

She boarded the bus without looking back. Those already on board were struck by the pitiful sight of the young girl entering the bus with her long black plaits wearing a faded dress that had seen better days. She looked far too young, her face too hardened, her eyes too focused and far too alone in the world. Little did they know that in her heart she felt a force guiding her, propelling her forward.

Her feet were already aching in those hand-me-down shoes. She opened her bag, took her old flip-flops out, freed her feet and settled in her seat, looking out of the window. She would forever carry a pair of flip-flops in her bag wherever she went, freeing her rough toes at the earliest opportunity.

For a moment, all her fears disappeared, eclipsed by the beauty of the countryside she was leaving behind as the bus moved fast towards São Paulo. She opened the window to feel the warm air on her hair and her face, and to hear the bird songs.

She arrived at Estacao da Luz in the centre of São Paulo at just thirteen years of age. She had nothing but her sister's address and a fierce determination to escape what she had left behind. But the beautifully written letters did not tell the sad truth of the difficulties Maria was facing in the capital.

I often try to imagine what she felt arriving in São Paulo among the noise and chaos inherent of big cities. Did she feel afraid? Overwhelmed? The times I asked her that question she simply replied: 'No, I did not feel any of these things, I felt glad to be away and I knew deep down that I was there to find work and that I would help my parents and surviving siblings.' I never heard or witnessed her show any sign of weakness.

I have a feeling that by the age of thirteen, she had already witnessed and experienced so much suffering that she was ready for anything. But my guess is that there existed in her an unexplainable force, an illogical intuition that guided her throughout her life. When her intuitive force kicked in, she was unstoppable.

On her arrival, she showed the bus driver a piece of paper with Maria's address on it. He helped her find her way to her sister's lodgings.

Maria stopped, open-mouthed, when she saw Iracy arriving with a small bag of belongings and a huge grin on her face. Iracy's heart missed a beat at the sight of Maria – her elder sister who had also been a mother to her.

It became clear that her sister shared a room with an unpleasant guy in a guest house full of migrants from many different rural areas of Brazil. He was called Toninho. At first Iracy assumed that he had a speech impediment with the way he slurred his words and his difficulty stringing in his sentences together. But what surprised her the most was the dismissive way he treated her sister. She disliked him instantly. However, for some unexplainable reason, Maria loved him very much, always fussing around him, walking on eggshells.

Now she finally understood what people meant when they said that love was blind, but it seemed to her that love was also extremely stupid.

Maria made her young sister a bed on the floor and told her to be very quiet or she would be in a lot of trouble with the landlady. She stayed there for a couple of nights determined to get a job and get out of her sister's way. One night she heard Toninho whispering to Maria: 'Now you have an extra mouth to feed you'd better get more shifts, even if it means working day and night.'

Cursing him under her breath, Iracy felt an immense sadness for her beloved sister. In her mind she could not conceive why anyone would treat Maria like this. It was even more difficult to comprehend why Maria allowed herself to be treated in such a way. Yes, she thought, love was blind and very stupid indeed.

The next morning, young Iracy woke up at the crack of dawn. Humming a little tune, she got dressed fast and walked to a newspaper stand in town and asked the owner to help her with the job ads in the local paper. He was impressed by her determination and soon circled some possible positions, such as a nanny or companion. After some disastrous interviews she managed to secure a live-in position caring for an elderly lady.

She stayed in this job for several years. The lady was kind, really liked her and helped her with her reading and writing and taught her how to move around the city. She went back to her sister and proudly announced, in front of Toninho:

'I have found a live-in position. I don't need to stay here anymore, after all, you have one lazy, drunk bastard to keep – he is only good at writing soppy letters.'

'What letters?' he asked, confused.

It would take a lifetime of suffering, and the greatest loss of her life, before Maria's love for him finally evaporated from her heart and she mastered the courage to throw him out.

Iracy gave Maria a hug that lasted an eternity. There was so much she wanted to say to her sister, but she knew there was nothing she could do or say to make her sister see sense, to make her know her worth, to make her appreciate how amazing she was, to make her wake up and throw Toninho out.

'Maria, I will be back on my day off. Here is the address and the lady's phone number if you need me for anything.'

She walked out of the house with a spring in her step; she was relieved to get out of her sister's way, excited to start her new job. She also left wondering who had written those soppy letters glamourising Maria's life in São Paulo.

On the third Sunday of the month, her only day off, she had one desire – to spend her day of freedom with Maria. She would put up with Toninho, she would hold her tongue. Her day off was to be spent sharing, dreaming and scheming with her sister.

Maria rented a small room in a large Portuguese colonial-style house surrounded by verandas. Once painted a dark, vibrant shade of green, it was now looking rundown. Years of dust had settled on the veranda and almost all the window shutters were broken, giving it that haunted, lonely appearance of neglect. It was hard to imagine who lived there, or if anyone, apart from ghosts, mice, stray cats and dogs, lived there at all. It was in the middle of one of São Paulo's busiest and dirtiest streets. The noise and chaos of the traffic that made Iracy feel slightly frightened and overwhelmed was now, three years from her arrival, simply background noise.

She had started to develop a longing for the silence of Serrania: the smell of the hot earth, the starry night skies throwing down those streaks of lights that looked like stars falling to Earth – the shooting stars. As a young girl on those hot nights, she would lay on the grass and gaze at the midnight-blue canvas above, watching the shooting stars, imagining she could catch them with her hands. As she caught them, she made impossible wishes, dreaming dreams as big as her imagination. But it was the bird songs she missed the most; she loved listening intently to them and guessing the name of each bird. How much longer could her memory retain the lovely sounds of each bird?

Well before she got to the house, she could see her sister dressed in her glad rags ready to take her to church, for she had now been converted to the Assembly of God. This time, Maria was not alone: standing next to her was a very well-dressed man with a superior air about him, smoking a cigarette. As she approached, she noticed that he was different from any of the migrants she had met before. She panicked, assuming he was yet another unscrupulous landlord she had heard about coming to put up the rent with vile threats of eviction.

She hugged her sister and tried to ignore the stranger but from the corner of her eye she could take in his beauty: jet black curls falling down his forehead, broad strong shoulders. But what she found most intriguing and striking were his eyes. They were two pools of darkness that gave away the despair his smiling mocking lips were trying to hide. He stubbed his cigarette with his perfectly polished shining black shoe then turned to her.

'I see … this is what the fuss is all about? Your sister has been nervously waiting for your arrival since the early hours, now I know why, you're hardly a girl about town, I can see the straw under your ears,' and he laughed.

'And who do you think you are, Mister?' she said, 'an arrogant, pompous city boy no doubt!'

He laughed this time, a full belly laugh. That girl had spirit. He was not used to being put in his place.

'City boy?' Maria laughed at him. 'He is no better than us, he is from rural São Paulo.'

'That may be so, but not any rural backwards place like Serrania, no, no, I am from Batatais!'

Maria and Iracy burst out laughing.

He went on, 'You see, Batatais is the land of the potato. There, the most amazing potatoes are grown by educated, cultured farmers. We have the best schools, the best teachers, the most cultured and well-educated children. Let me tell you about the beauty of that land. Flowing rivers, waterfalls, potato fields that stretch for miles.'

At this point Maria and Iracy were laughing so hard they were holding their bellies.

'Not a city boy then, just a potato boy!!' Iracy shouted, catching her breath from too much laughter. They carried on mocking him with no mercy.

'Crazy stupid illiterate *mineiras*, what do you know?' They could tell he was offended. He lit another cigarette and sulked.

'How dare you, little shit, call my sister illiterate! She can read and write. She walked for miles for well over two years to attend school. Watch your mouth.'

They left him sulking.

They had so much to share, so much to dream about together. Although Maria had reservations about bringing the entire family to São Paulo, Iracy's unfaltering determination and energy kept her going, allowing her to dream a little too.

'Iracy, my name is Odecio by the way, with an O … Odecio. Your ignorant sister has no manners and has not introduced us properly.'

They walked away from him fast, laughing and shouting.

'Odecio with an O, potato boy, potato boy!'

He could hear the echoes of their laughter in the distance.

'Ha ha ha ha!' really meant delicious laughter.

Iracy was sixteen but still looked thirteen, with the same long plaits, white socks and worn-out little dresses from Serrania.

Odecio was twenty but looked older, sophisticated, knowing. It was as if he had already lived many lives. But it was his troubled eyes that would haunt her forever.

No one can really know what is behind a tear

Several years had passed since that lucky day when Iracy went searching for work, landing a job that met her needs at the time, allowing her to take another step with her tiny rural feet towards her master plan.

The work was easy, her boss – a sweet lady with a kind soul – was so different from her previous boss. They got on well. Iracy would go beyond the call of duty to assist her in the many daily tasks required to run a home. She would also care for her when she felt unwell. She told her stories of her life back in Serrania. The old lady would be amused about her siblings' constant squabbles and saddened by their plight. She would ask Iracy to read to her, using the opportunity to correct her and teach her.

But the most precious gift Iracy brought her was empathic companionship and bringing her closer to her grandchildren who, because of Iracy, were glad to make their visits more frequent and a lot longer. Iracy was a natural with them, able to amuse them and discipline them when necessary.

But despite the comfort of her surroundings, food like she had never seen before and being treated with kindness, young Iracy felt lonely. She missed her mum and her siblings; she constantly worried about them, often waking up from nightmares when her mum was ill, or another sibling was being buried.

The only thing that kept her going was the certainty she had that one day soon she would have enough money to rent a house and bring them all to São Paulo.

Then one day, just like that, with no drama, no pain, no fuss, her boss took her final breath.

Iracy never panicked in the face of death or tragedy. She was always able to keep her cool. No hysterical display of grief for her. At times like these, she sprang into action.

Her first action was to kneel down close to the old lady and say a little prayer:

'Sainted Angel of the Lord, my zealous guardian, please keep this dear lady's soul. May you find her a place by your side, she was a good woman, never hurt anyone and gave me a job and a home when I had nowhere to go. While you are at it, don't forget I am now jobless, soon to be homeless again.'

She covered the lady up with a blanket, stroking her hair, kissing her forehead and looked for the instructions she was given by the family in case of emergencies.

Following the instructions she received when she took the job, she left the house, walked to the bakery next door, and informed the owner. He took care of everything and in no time at all the family arrived, the body was taken, and the funeral was arranged for that same night.

On that night, after Iracy and everyone had absorbed the shock and were paying their respects to the deceased lady's body laid in an open mahogany coffin with golden handles in her front room, the lady's daughter found Iracy crying in the kitchen while making coffee for everyone. She was touched by her fondness for her mother, despite being there just over three years. She had heard her mother speak fondly of the girl from Serrania who had impressed her with her work ethic, her ability to learn fast, how her grandchildren had taken to her and how genuinely kind and precise she was in her mother's care. What the daughter could not have known was that Iracy was mainly crying for the job she had, for the only security she had in the world.

Now the plan, the master of all plans, was in jeopardy. Her heart sunk, her hopes and dreams now seemed only a silly idea in a young girl's heart. She looked truly sad, even sadder than the lady's flesh and blood.

During the funeral, Iracy took care of the young grandchildren. They loved her, she was fun yet efficient and practical in their care. She read them stories, made sure they ate properly and took no nonsense from them.

The children were also crying now that the visits to their grandmother, made all that much more appealing due to Iracy's presence, were over.

When the last guests said their goodbyes to the family, she was approached by the lady's daughter and offered a job as the grandchildren's nanny. She could live in or out. She was offered much better pay and two whole Sundays off a month. Although Iracy was aware that a stupid, wide grin had spread all over her face, she tried to maintain her bereaved composure in front of the family.

Seven little graves, seven empty holes in a tiny mother's heart

In just over three years, Iracy had managed to save enough money to bring her remaining family to São Paulo. She found the older ones jobs, and the young ones schools. She rented a tiny house for them all. She was earning enough, living in and hardly spending any money on herself. Although she was beautiful, and blessed with a slim figure, strong straight black hair, soft brown complexion, generous bow shaped lips and dark eyes, Iracy was never vain. She had inherited her grandmother's indigenous genes, and no one knows why she was the only child to be given an ancient Tupi-Guarani name. The external never interested her that much.

She was blessed with a powerful determination to act, an intuition that guided her throughout her life and a soul that could see right through people's hearts no matter how hard they tried to hide. In my darkest hour, already in her sixties, it was her that was by my side: a series of unfortunate events almost took my will to get up in the morning and breathe in and out; she jumped on an airplane for the first time in her life and travelled 10,000 miles all by herself, against doctors' orders, to comfort me, sharing her wisdom, sharing her strength, quietly and decidedly teaching me how to heal.

'Iracy, think twice before boarding that plane, you could die on the way there,' Odecio, her sisters and relatives tried to persuade her not to go.

'If I do, my daughter will know I was making my way to her, and this will give her strength to carry on.'

Joao Inacio, Francisca, my beloved *vovó* Chiquinha, and their remaining children were all being pulled by Iracy's magnetic force. She was calling them, urging them to leave Serrania behind; her eight remaining siblings would not die of malnutrition, would grow strong thus giving their own offspring a better chance to live to a ripe old age under polluted skies. Enough was enough!

A lifetime had passed since that baking hot Sunday when Joao Inacio knocked on the door of that indigenous woman with a reputation, looking for a wife. Francisca was now a wife and a mother of so many children in her own right. However, the prospect of abandoning her life in Serrania to travel to an unknown metropolis, taking all her children with her, filled her with dread: she once again felt like the young girl who had left home to marry a stranger so much older than her, all those years ago. Life in Serrania was brutal: her life constituted trying to appease her husband's temper, which grew worse every day, doing endless chores and taking care of the children that never stopped coming. She was either pregnant, recovering from labour, nursing a baby, grieving for the loss of yet another child, or both. Every time a child died, she died a little more inside, leaving that familiar cavernous emptiness that slowly became a part of her. But it was the guilt she felt for not being able to save them that weighed heavily on her heart. Yet there were joyful moments with Joao. She knew he cared for her. The children delighted her, made her laugh, made her heart heal a little, even overflow at times. This was her life, the only life she knew. Leaving it all behind to travel to São Paulo was a scary thought. But Joao was right, the work was getting scarce, they had too many mouths to feed.

At dawn, on the big day of departure, while they all slept and dreamt dreams of infinite possibilities, my beloved *vovó* Chiquinha – Francisca – went to see the minute graves of the children she could not save, those she could not protect. Seven little babies, seven empty holes in a tiny mother's heart.

'I am sorry, I am so sorry I have to go, I can't take you with me. Change is coming in the back of the wind ...' And the seven empty holes in her heart began to fill with seven little ghosts; she relived their tiny feet and hands at birth, their faces, the sound of their gurgling, their cries ...

seven little ghosts
seven spirit children
went with her
trying to forever fill
seven empty holes in a tiny mother's
heart.

And her ancestors, the magnificent Tupi people, who once lived dignified existences on that very same hot, terracotta soil, under that very same clear blue sky and scorching sun, screamed so loud that the wind of change howled, the skies darkened, the heavens opened, and it rained in Serrania for seven days.

'It always seems impossible until it's done.' – Nelson Mandela

The howling wind of change catapulted Joao Inacio, Francisca and their children all the way to the capital of São Paulo. They arrived on a stormy Sunday morning. Iracy and Maria got up at the crack of dawn, dusted down their glad rags, put on their best hats and packed their handbags to meet their parents and siblings. Even Iracy made an unusual effort for the occasion; she was wearing a new dress, a pair of shoes and a posh handbag containing a bag of sugar-coated peanuts for her siblings and a pair of worn-out flip-flops for her tiny rural feet. She now wore her hair up, with a touch of rouge and lipstick. At eighteen she no longer looked like the young teenager that left Serrania. She was older; she carried herself with a confident and sophisticated air.

With her head held high, she could feel her heartbeat … every single beat pounding in her chest … hard and loud.

Maria could not contain her excitement. She felt anxious. She feared what they would think of her, of her fella, of her new life. She feared how things would work out. She feared everything, even life itself.

Iracy had managed to rent a small house for them all but there was hardly any furniture in it yet. Maria wished she could be a little bit more like her younger sister. Nothing seemed to phase her. She lived with incredible trust.

'Don't worry about the lack of furniture, Maria, things will work out. They have a roof over their heads, mattresses on the floor, a few saucepans and a cupboard full of food to last them a week.'

At 11.30 am, the bus arrived at Estacao da Luz. The same bus that, not so long ago, had carried Maria and Iracy away from their parents, their siblings and everything they knew.

Maria jumped up in excitement when she saw them getting off the bus, welling up, trying hard to compose herself.

Iracy was shocked at the sight of her parents. They looked so much older, so much poorer. Francisca had developed a bit of a hunchback and walked with some difficulty with shallow breaths. Joao Inacio seemed totally lost, looking around at the chaos of traffic, the sea of people; the sounds of the city with its constant cry of sirens and car horns disorientated him. He squeezed Francisca's hand, not so much to protect her but for his own reassurance.

The siblings walked behind their parents as if seeking shelter, their astounded eyes – bombarded with so many stimuli – darting everywhere. The only one who stood out from the crowd, with her nose up, already full of airs and graces, was Ana Maria Luisa. Oh my! She had grown up in the last few years, no longer the waif with a runny nose always scratching away the lice that seemed to love her thick head of hair.

'*Mamae*, *Papai*, boys, girls, Ana Maria Luisa, over here, over here,' Iracy screamed.

The pitiful party stopped and stared at the well-dressed sisters waving at them.

They all ran towards each other; time and place dissolved as Maria and Iracy embraced their parents and siblings. In that moment, the fears of the city, filled with pedestrians walking on concrete slabs, and the unfamiliar smell of exhaust from thousands of cars, disappeared from their hearts as they gave in to the contagious emotions of being reunited.

They wandered on, as if in a surreal dream, mixing in with São Paulo's Sea of people. New faces flashed past them: pale, painted, dark, tired, happy and sad faces dazzling past. Ana Maria Luisa watched them all, heard them all, and feared nothing.

The Assembly of God

The Assemblies of God, I was later to discover, were a group of over 140 churches around the world, which together formed the world's largest Pentecostal faith community, followed by over 67 million devotees around the world.

They followed the Bible and had an authority, rule of faith and strict conduct. When I was growing up, women were not allowed to cut their hair, wear make-up or paint their nails. Members of the Assembly were not allowed to listen to the radio or watch TV. Things are a little more relaxed now.

The Assembly of God assembled the poor, the needy, the lost, the lonely, the righteous, the devious, and the greedy. It provided shelter for all aspects of human nature, once a week, in the name of the Lord. Some were true to their intentions and tried to adopt the pastor's teachings, some attempted to tame their dark side and some never saw their shadow lurking behind them as they committed atrocious acts in the name of the Lord.

When they arrived in São Paulo with their mixed faith of imposed Catholicism and inherited indigenous beliefs, members of the Assembly of God paid the family a visit. They helped my grandparents by taking them kind gifts of bits of furniture, clothes, shoes, food and of course a Bible for each member the family. The fact that most of them could hardly read was just a small detail in the greater scheme of things.

And on the seventh day, they repaid all that kindness by joining the Church. Most of my aunties and uncles stayed true to this Church for the rest of their lives. In some ways, it saved them and their children from a life of crime and addiction on the streets of São Paulo.

As my parents left the Church before I was born, I was never a devout member of the Assembly of God. I have vivid memories of attending the church with my aunties and cousins. I loved my time with them. I prayed before meals, before bedtime, and prayed at the church. But I always felt like a sinner. My skirts were too short, my hair not long enough, my laugh a little too loud, my childish innocent jokes were things of the devil, learnt by faithless children being brought up by faithless parents. I was a seven-year-old sinner.

Still, I loved the warmth and care my aunties had for me. I was received with such excitement by my cousins. I was their only female faithless cousin, full of games and stories from the outside world. When they were not teaching me the Bible, and when their parents were out of sight, they were eager to hear the latest songs being played on the radio, the stories, and the silly jokes. We had such fun for hours and hours. We would sing hymns that would rapidly change into a pop tune and for some bizarre reason we would pretend to speak in tongues, just like the grown-ups did in church when possessed by the Holy Spirit.

> *Asha Ta Ta It*
> *Ka La Ma Sha Ki*
> *Si Ki Li Ba Ba*

Trying to outdo each other with more and more ridiculous, meaningless sounds and wetting ourselves with so much laughter.

My time at my aunties' houses evokes memories and soul-stirring feelings that I will treasure forever. On the days that we went to visit Auntie Orminda, we got up early as it took two buses to get there. I was always in a state of excitement during those visits. I treasured every second of the adventure. She and her husband, Uncle Aristide, had somehow managed to buy a plot of land in one of São Paulo's suburbs. He was a builder, and she was a cleaner at a local hospital.

Every time we arrived, she was covered in dust or paint, helping to build the house. Once we found her on top of the roof singing a tune and banging away with her hammer and nails.

As they could not afford builders, and Aristide had to work during the day, she started and finished a lot of the building work herself.

Nothing seemed to faze her. I remember when the building work was well under way – in addition to building a basic family home they also built several little houses to rent and to house their children's future families. During that time of intense and backbreaking labour, her husband became absent, always working late somewhere. The truth finally came to the surface when my auntie found the rascal in one of the half-built houses, in the arms of another woman. She beat the woman up, threw her on the streets, grabbed her husband and placed him back in the marital bed. The matter was thus resolved. There was no mention of divorce, or couple's therapy, or great drama. She claimed what she felt was rightfully hers and life went on.

She cried to Iracy and was offered some wisdom on the matter.

'Orminda, men are like dogs, they need to know who the boss is, you are too soft and soppy with Aristides, try and keep him in line and don't ever waste your tears on a man.'

With one sentence she tarnished every single man. The strong, the weak, the noble and the wicked. I felt she had her reasons to feel that way for she had witnessed too much cruelty and not enough kindness to form a more balanced view of the opposite sex.

I remember my auntie and uncle being very close in their later years. Auntie Orminda died young from a heart condition. Aristide was put in a home. Iracy would visit him, and he would hold her hand and call her Orminda. She played the game. He lost all awareness that his wife was, in fact, dead. Perhaps it was the only way he could bear her absence.

Orminda had a special way of making each of us feel welcome and loved. She was high-spirited, always so pleased to see us, and took a real interest in what was going on with each of us, however trivial. These two sisters got on like a house on fire. They shared deep secrets, a rich history that they loved to relive, and Orminda cried at their past losses and current troubles. This would soon turn into laughter. They laughed out loud at anything and everything.

Mum would give us some old clothes to change into and we would run around the plot of land, climbing trees and playing in the building works with our cousins. Frantically and happily, we would play for hours, only stopping when called for lunch or cake.

When Odecio visited Auntie Orminda with us on Sundays, there was always a great dynamic between the two couples. The first thing Orminda would do was boil the water to make fresh coffee, fetch fresh bread and bring out her delicious cake. Always the *fuba* cake, made from maize. This was how my mum, and my aunties showed their love. Cake love. *Fuba* cake love.

But my mum's *fuba* cake was the best! Whenever I visited, she would slip a whole freshly baked *fuba* cake in my suitcase when I was packing to return home. The *fuba* cake, filled with so much love, arrived a bit squashed after a twelve-hour flight but was nevertheless devoured by my husband and kids within minutes of my arrival back in England.

During our Sunday visits to Auntie Orminda's house, Odecio would quickly hide the kettle or her cake tin. She would always make the same little speech.

'I am bursting with happiness with all of you here. I will go boil some water and fetch the *fuba* cake.' All proud of herself. We would hear her frantically looking everywhere for her things.

'What? Where has the kettle gone? Where is my cake tin? Odecio!' She would shout and come running in with a broom stick to get him.

'You rascal, wicked wicked man, give me my things back.'

Odecio would laugh, deny all knowledge; we would all fall about laughing and she would hit him with her broom, showing no mercy until he gave her things back.

She was a remarkable woman. She had five sons and was always trying to produce a daughter.

One day at the hospital, performing her endless cleaning duties, she heard the nurses commenting about the sad fate of a premature little girl. Her mother, a drug addict, had just given birth to her and asked the midwives to take her away and do whatever they wished with her. She never saw her daughter.

Orminda dropped her mop into her bucket and walked to the nursery. She was confronted with the lamentable sight of the abandoned waif, breathing with difficulty through various tubes trying to keep her alive, inside an incubator that seemed gigantic against her small frame.

'Look at you, beautiful little baby girl. You are special and loved and I know you will grow to be strong and enjoy the wonder that life is.'

No one knows how long she stayed there talking to the premature baby girl and saying endless prayers to God. What I know is that the nurses and staff working in the premature baby unit did not stop her and allowed her all the time she needed with that baby. I feel that they were moved by Orminda's show of love. They also knew that all the other babies in the unit had their mothers with them, praying for them and without Orminda's tears and prayers that baby would possibly die without ever receiving an ounce of love.

In her usual tomboyish manner, she walked from the premature baby unit straight to the secretary of the hospital director.

'Can I see the director please?'

'Who shall I say is here for him?'

'Orminda, the hospital cleaner, here about an adoption.'

After much pleading, he allowed her to adopt the baby girl. She called her Raquel.

One of our most exciting visits to Auntie Orminda's was when we went to meet Raquel. She looked unreal to me, her translucent skin, pink scalp and not yet fully formed fingernails stirred, even in me, a need to protect her. Orminda was glowing with happiness and purpose.

'Look Iracy, God sent me my girl. She is here now.'

We all took turns to hold her, to sing to her, and to give her all the love her mum was not able to give her.

Against all odds, that premature little girl survived. She grew up to be blonde with striking green eyes, so vastly different from us all, but only on the outside.

Let the fun begin

Joao, Francisca and the remaining siblings were now living in a São Paulo district called Vila Maria. Despite having to sleep on mattresses on the floor with her sisters and queue for the one outside bathroom, Iracy never felt happier. She was home. She had been so lonely at the lady's house, despite having her own en suite room and beautiful surroundings. Loneliness seemed to her even worse than poverty. They didn't fight too much, forgave quickly, and had each other's back. The only major concern for her parents was Anna Maria Luisa. Since arriving in São Paulo, she had changed from a young country teenager into a modern Paulista. She would not give her full wages to her mum, keeping some back for her red lipsticks, outrageously colourful dresses and high heels. She was even beginning to go to the hairdressers and was wearing her hair shorter and more stylish. The folks at the Assembly of God had noticed and some were already gossiping; some were giving her the eye of disapproval. She didn't notice them but continued to greet and treat them with her usual openness of heart and gregarious nature.

When the sisters managed to get time off together, they would spend it with Maria who still lived at her lodgings with her boyfriend. It was much more fun there with the opportunity to flirt and have a laugh with the other migrants.

One Sunday they heard a funfair was coming into town all the way from Rio de Janeiro. The excitement was high among the young migrants. Iracy asked Maria about Odecio, whom she had not seen for a while. Maria explained that he was getting busy with his business as a car mechanic and was often called away to rescue cars. Maria told her he loved cars and had trained himself as a mechanic and apparently was extremely good at it. He was going up in the world. The clever duck: reaching deep in her apron pocket, Maria handed Iracy a note.

'Go on, read it, it is from him.'

She opened the note and immediately recognised the handwriting. It was Odecio who had written all those letters on Maria's behalf! It was his imagination and his poetic writing that made Maria's life in São Paulo seem so grand. The clever duck.

Hello Iracy,

Maria has been keeping me up to date. I heard the big guy upstairs has been closing and opening doors for you. I am glad you are back with your family. You are lucky to have them around you.

I have been very busy and getting more and more clients, São Paulo's rich are buying cars, and they need me. Ha ha! I want their dosh.

I would love it if you could come to the funfair with me. I heard it is a big one, but it will not be as big or fancy as the ones in Batatais. I can assure you of that.

Odecio

Hello Odecio,

Thank you for your letter and, by the way, all the others you wrote for Maria. I have also been kept updated of your whereabouts. Rumour has it that you are a drunk and a womaniser. And the way you speak of our God is shameful. I am now a devout member of the Assembly of God; I have no interest in funfairs and could not be seen with a sinner like you.

Iracy

Iracy's reply hurt him on so many levels. The rejection, the rudeness of her reply and her judgement of him. But most of all he was angry at the Assembly of God and all the other Christian Protestant churches popping up all over São Paulo. He hated the way religion oppressed the poor. He was reading Karl Marx and that made so much more sense to him. He became a communist. He suffered with the injustice he saw around him. He never changed until his dying day. He had true compassion for the poor, the oppressed, the lost, the lonely. I am sure he could see himself in all of them. But she wasn't entirely wrong; he liked a drink too much and the bottle was sometimes his best friend and, although he was no womaniser, he appreciated the female form and loved female attention.

I loved hearing his stories about his girlfriends before he was committed to my mother. He used to brag that he was very handsome and popular with the ladies back in the day. He shared that he went out with a girl of German descent who introduced him to her parents. The girl's father was so surprised by the deep black tone of his hair that he took Odecio outside and made him wash it several times in a horse's trough in front of the whole family to prove he did not dye his hair.

A few weeks after their correspondence, he saw Iracy again and this time with her sister, Luisa. He could not take his eyes off Luisa: her body confidence, the way she dressed and wore her hair took him by surprise. He could tell she was free-spirited with a fire in her belly. As Iracy continued to ignore him, he asked Luisa to go to the fair with him.

'Hello, I am Odecio with an 'o'. It is lovely to meet you.' He hesitated for a moment then blurted out, 'would you like to come to the fair with me?'

'Yes', she said, looking him straight in the eye. One word. *Yes.* But the smile on her lips and the look on her face spoke many forbidden words to that young man's heart.

Iracy was taken aback at the turn of events but said nothing. She had a way of hiding her emotions, always appearing in control even of the most tragic of situations, silently planning her next move and deadly blows.

The following Sunday, with just two weeks until the fair arrived, she met Odecio's brother, Celsio, at Maria's lodgings. He was taller than Odecio, not as handsome but calmer and more of an introvert. She chatted with him about Batatais, and they both laughed at Odecio's grandiose description of his home town. On an impulse, she asked him to take her to the funfair. Taken aback he said, 'Sure.'

'I have nothing to wear so you will have to buy me a dress.'

'Ok, why don't we walk to the market now.'

They walked together chatting. She picked two dresses like the ones Luisa had been wearing and asked him to choose one, but he was unsure: 'I'm afraid of choosing the wrong one.'

'In that case I will have both.'

On the evening of the funfair, Iracy and Luisa arrived early at Maria's, carrying bags with their outfits, and a paraphernalia of hair and make-up things. Luisa was delighted to do Iracy's hair and make-up. In no time at all, she was transformed. She looked in the mirror and pulled a terrified face.

'Dear God, Ana Maria Luisa, this is not me!'

'Nonsense, you look beautiful, striking, a proper young woman of the city of São Paulo.'

With a little trepidation, dressed to the nines, Luisa carrying herself with enviable confidence whilst Iracy, a little unsure, feeling like she was wearing fancy dress for a pantomime, struggling to walk on such high heels, went downstairs to the front of the house to meet their respective dates. Odecio's jaw dropped when he saw Iracy, then the penny dropped, and he shouted angrily at her.

'You turn me down with all that saintly talk about God and you are going with my brother? Come on, Luisa, let's get out of here, you look amazing, and I need a drink.'

Iracy ignored him, grabbing Celsio's arm. 'We'd better be going ourselves.'

The fair was much more than her imagination had been telling her all those weeks. She loved the rides, the music, the bright lights, the candy floss, the sugar-coated peanuts, the toffee apples, and the laughter coming from happy faces. The energy was electrifying. This was Iracy's first taste of fairy tale and carefree fun. She was drunk with the atmosphere. Celsio was gentle, not pushy, and seemed happy.

Odecio had been drinking as he always did to hide some upset or another. A bit tipsy and hand in hand with Luisa, he spotted Celsio and Iracy, arm in arm. He launched into his brother, throwing the first punch. Before long, the two brothers were wrestling on the floor. Iracy looked down at Odecio, pleased with herself. She had him right there in the palm of her hands. And there he would stay for the rest of his life.

She grabbed Luisa. 'Let's go home, Luisa. Mum will be worried.'

'No way, I am having fun and I am not letting your little scheme here spoil it for me.'

Luisa disappeared into the crowd. Iracy went home and when she got there everyone was fast asleep. She took her make-up off and put her nightdress on, careful not to wake her siblings up. She flopped down onto the mattress on the floor. But she could not sleep, worrying about Luisa. Little did she know that she did not need to worry about that one.

Luisa decided to leave Iracy, Odecio and that brother of his to their own devices. Let them squabble, struggle and suffer in dramas of their own making. Nothing to do with me, she thought. She walked on without a care in the world. She was blessed with the ability to truly live in the moment, if the moment was good and pleased her of course. And that moment was delicious. She was savoring every split of every tiny second.

She breathed in the air, sticking her tongue out to taste the sweet smell coming out of the stalls; she looked at the boys and girls making toffee apples and candy floss at the speed of light, desperately trying to keep the queues down.

She realised she had never tasted candy floss. She jumped the queue and went right up to the guy in charge.

'My boyfriend bought me a candy floss, he handed the right money to that young boy over there, I have been waiting here for almost an hour, can you please hand me some?' Before the stall owner could protest or question her further, she added: 'yes, my boyfriend is just over there, he is part of security. Shall I call him over to clarify things for you, Sir?'

She walked away with a huge grin on her red lips, savoring every tiny bite of her pink and white, fluffy and sweet-smelling candy floss. 'Wow, it is just as delicious as it looks,' she muttered to herself.

She walked from stall to stall, mingling with the crowd, singing and swinging her hips to the music lost in a dream …

He spotted her from a distance. He first noticed her face – round, only slightly tanned, mixed-race…may be not, the face too pale and the eyes more like Tupi eyes … a bit drunk by the way she was walking barefoot, swinging her red shoes over one shoulder. And that dress. Showing her bare shoulders, a full skirt patterned with crimson roses. But it was the way she was savoring her candy floss, ever so slowly, trying to make it last, that intrigued him the most.

He shouted to his boss. 'I need to take a break.'

He left the go-carts he oversaw and ran quickly towards her. 'Hey, your candy floss is nearly over, can I buy you another one?'

She turned around, completely ignored him, and walked on, grinning to herself in her full power.

'A toffee apple then?'

She turned around and slapped his face, hard.

'Wow, what was that for, little lady?'

'One, I am not a little lady and two, do you always go racing after young girls offering them sweet treats? What kind of a man are you? If one can even call you a man. Now run along and let me enjoy the last hour of the fair.'

He walked away nursing his bruised ego.

But his face was now imprinted in her brain. She relived the sound of his voice – deep, strong, resolved – the mischief in his eyes, and his smile. Something stirred within her. Not knowing quite what to do, she carried on walking, luxuriating in everything, especially the small details of her encounter with the stranger.

Lost in her dream, she failed to realise that the fair was becoming empty, with people making their way home and the workers packing their stalls.

'I am sorry if I came across as arrogant and upset you.'

With her heart racing, she turned around, but this time she was less afraid of this stranger standing in front of her, wearing his heart on his sleeve, looking apologetic and a touch lost.

'Apologies accepted. I am new here in São Paulo, my sister warned me to take care of myself.' She offered her hand and smiled. 'Ana Maria Luisa from Serrania, Minas Gerais. How do you do?'

He took her hand, all sticky and sweet-smelling and kissed it.

'Mauricio, from every part of this land, funfair worker and traveler.'

'Do you mean you just travel around with the funfair?'

'Yes, Ma'am, since I was a boy, my whole family works and lives this way.'

She was fascinated and started bombarding him with questions. He walked with her to his motorhome, making her wait outside. He came back with a couple of chairs, a throw, which he put around her shoulders, hot coffee, two baguettes filled with different cheeses and salad; he also gifted her a huge bar of chocolate.

They sat there sharing the food, the coffee, the chocolate, their stories and their dreams …

He learnt she was just seventeen, she learnt he was twenty-two.

'Yeah, I love this life, but it can be lonely. I have never found someone to share this lifestyle with me. Young women need more security than this.'

'Well, I don't, I would love to live like this, travelling around, getting to know new places and opening the fair, turning on the lights, the music, the rides, making popcorn, toffee apples, hot dogs, candy floss. What a life that would be, bringing joy to people's miserable lives.'

'Will you marry me then? You get it, you totally get me, and I have already fallen in love with you, Ana Maria Luisa from Serrania, Minas Gerais.'

'Yes, I will Mauricio from every part of this land, funfair worker and traveler,' and she laughed out loud at the crazy idea.

They realised that the night was disappearing before them. They noticed the first flashes of sunbeams trying to come through the fading night sky.

They looked at each other.

At that moment, Ana Maria Luisa had an out-of-body experience: she saw herself standing at the crossroads of her young life. If she stayed, she knew perfectly well what was in store for her: a life of hard work, a life of duty, a life where her nature would have to be silenced by the Church, by the fears of others around her. Fears that were not her own.

'Find me a job here, Mauricio. Teach me the ropes, I am coming with you.'

Just before dawn Iracy heard Luisa quietly getting onto her mattress. She was still dressed, bright-eyed, with a defiant look that scared Iracy.

'Luisa, you are scaring me, where have you been? Get a grip, the fair is over.'

'Iracy, I have found the love of my life, I am leaving in a few hours with him.'

'Has Odecio filled with your head with nonsense? Girls like us are eternal Cinderellas who will never be chosen by a prince, Luisa. Just frogs, sometimes poisonous ones.'

Luisa whispered. 'Odecio has nothing to do with this Iracy. In fact, he bored me with his lamentations about the way you treat him, apparently worse than a dog.' She stifled a giggle.

'Who then? Who Luisa?'

'Mau–ri–cio,' she said, pronouncing every syllable slowly in an intoxicated way, 'he oversaw the go-carts tonight. He works for the funfair company and can operate all the rides, fix them, assemble them and put them down again – a genius, I am telling you. He already found me a job at the fair. I can't, I just can't be left behind, watching all the rides being packed away, moving on leaving behind nothing but dust and litter, longing for it to come back next year, going back to normal life. Can't you understand?'

'You can't do this; you will break Mum's heart. What about your job, where will you live? Mum and Dad will be humiliated at the Assembly of God.'

'Please cover for me Iracy,' she giggled making dramatic gestures, 'tell *Mamae* an angel has come for me, and chosen her very own Ana Maria Luisa to join the funfair travelling company and make people happy. Then some other time you can gently mention Mauricio – he is the one, my heart does not lie, we will be getting married very soon too. I want to be the one always moving on, always at the funfair, making people happy, being happy.' She went on, 'He is a good guy, he's got a kind heart, we talked all night. We share the same dreams.'

'You only met him a few hours ago! When will I see you? How will I know you are fine? Luisa, you are crazy!'

'I will find a way of getting letters to you all. And Iracy, open your eyes. Odecio is right, there are a lot of hypocrites, not so good Christians at the church. The preacher is getting richer every day. Odecio said that the preacher throws the collection money up in the air and what God doesn't catch he keeps for himself. Isn't Odecio funny?'

'Those poor credulous people can hardly afford to feed their children but no, he keeps taking their money every week. Manipulating their minds. If there is a God and I am his child, then he can see right through my heart, and he will care for me.' She quoted from the Bible:

So, do not fear, for I am with you; do not be dismayed, for I am your God. I will strengthen you and help you; I will uphold you with my righteous right hand.

Isaiah 41:10

'How clever of you, Ana Maria Luisa, manipulating the Lords' words to suit yourself!'

'Ha ha ha. Yes, I learnt from the preacher.' Ana Maria Luisa got up, gathered a few belongings ready to leave the house. Iracy jumped up from the mattress, and followed her out, it was already morning in Vila Maria, they could hear the first sounds of traffic humming in the distance. The sisters hugged for a long time, there was nothing else to say.

And just like that, taking her red lipsticked lips, her eager eyes, her dazzling dresses, her girly giggle with a head full of funfair dreams, and with Him right there beside her, she was gone.

Iracy went back to the house with a head full of worries and a hole in her heart. Her intuition was telling her that this fairy tale would not end with a happy ever after. But she was glad for her sister, let her love for now, laugh for now, be dazzling for now. Tomorrow would come soon enough.

A new sinner arrives to repent all his sins – Praise the Lord

But for Iracy, life went on. She walked past the grounds where the fair once was and noticed the dust and the litter they left behind and longed for it to come back next year and bring her sister back.

It was heart-breaking to tell her parents and siblings. They all cried, worried, felt angry, called her despicable names, and secretly felt a bit of envy at her courage to swim against the tide towards new adventures.

Iracy liked her day job; the night job was harder. There was always so much that needed doing at home – not only the endless domestic chores, but the emotional investment essential to keep each sibling doing their bit, going to school, to work, to church, not make Joao Inacio mad. His temper was getting worse and so was the wrath of his anger. The expectations put on him by the Church to have no one shaming his family, combined with the horror stories that frequently featured in the pastor's sermons, about the sinful lives of the São Paulo sinners, were beginning to take its toll on him. Luisa's audacity to elope with a sinner also contributed to his mental confusion. From the day he arrived at Estacao da Luz, until he took his final breath, he felt like a fish out of water and struggled to adapt.

His lowly-paid, brutal, manual job as a labourer at building sites was not helping either. Iracy also noticed how her mother's breathing was getting shallower, making it harder for her to breathe with each passing day.

She still visited her sister Maria, and chatted, teased, and fought with Odecio, usually over religious matters. But she was beginning to open her heart to him more and more. She shared that even if she wanted to go out with him, her mother could not take another heartbreak. The possibility of another daughter marrying outside of the Church would not go down too well. Even Maria was doing the decent thing and marrying her fella in church.

Odecio was fully aware of her dilemma. He admired her and how she looked after her family, always putting them first, giving all her wages to her mother. He felt grounded in her presence. Iracy, in turn, was proud of his work, the books he read and how altruistic he was to those less fortunate than himself.

Unknown to her, Odecio had been talking to Maria about joining the Church. Maria had explained that on the first Sunday of the month sinners could join the preacher at the altar and confess their sins; the preacher would then exorcise the Devil from the sinner. Some sinners would cry uncontrollably, others would even have fits, contorting their bodies while the Lord did his work. It was a good spectacle, and the church was always full on the first Sunday of the month. Once the Devil was truly exorcised, and the sinners repented all their sins, the congregation would go wild, sing loud, speak in tongues and the repented sinners would be welcomed into the Assembly of God. Odecio listened carefully to Maria's depiction, lost in thought, nodding occasionally.

One fine first Sunday of the month, a new sinner appeared at the altar. Iracy, who was sitting with her mum and siblings in the congregation, could not believe her eyes. There he was, Odecio, overdressed for the occasion as always. The grin on his face, that he was trying so hard to hide, did not fool her. She stared at him with critical eyes shaking her head from side to side as if to say, 'Don't you dare, Odecio, don't you dare.'

But he did dare. The preacher announced his name, sharing with the congregation that the young man in front of them wanted to be exorcised of all his sins. But when he was asked about his sins, Odecio froze and could not list them – as a forward-thinking rebellious young man he did not believe in sins, only circumstances; regaining his composure he said he drank and had fits of temper and he did not want the demon alcohol in his body anymore. He spoke with such a demanding tone that the congregation started singing, clapping, and shouting praise to the

Lord. The preacher then put both hands on Odecio's head, praying frantically with eyes shut; Odecio started to contort his body, throwing himself on the floor.

As the preacher started to shout his name 'Decio, Decio, you will be healed my child,' Iracy ran to the altar and shouted trying hard to be heard above the pandemonium.

'His name is Odecio with an O. Odecio.' He stopped contorting for a second winking at her, she smiled back.

He was not only accepted into the Church, but into her family with open arms.

Vovó Chiquinha adopted him and treated him like her son until the day she died.

He brought Iracy's family a lot of laughter, stories, and news from Europe about an imminent world war about to break out. He never arrived empty-handed. He brought fresh bread and meats, sweets, new shoes, and clothes for the young ones. They all loved him – the energy in the house rose tenfold when they heard his footsteps coming up the path, whistling and singing his sad songs of lost love and loss.

One evening when he had come to join them at dinner, Chiquinha shared with him that she would love to welcome his parents into her home one day soon. She was holding his secret that he was going to propose to Iracy very soon. He had told only Francisca, who was becoming a mother to him.

He became noticeably quiet, staring at his dinner. As if by magic, his larger-than-life presence started to shrink, and he appeared as deflated as a burst balloon. He looked like a lost little boy.

Trying to rescue the situation, Iracy told them he was an orphan and changed the subject. But her younger siblings were having none of it and begged him to tell his story.

The ugly truth of his life in glorious Batatais came to light. Her parents, her siblings listened wide-eyed and open-mouthed without interrupting him. His mother had been ill for months, with doctors, healers and witch doctors coming daily up and down the path to the house to no avail. One morning as he was leaving for school, he heard her calling his name very faintly. He walked into her bedroom, and she opened her arms to him.

'Come here my baby, you will always be my baby, my last child. I want you to remember how much I love you and how much I believe in you. Promise me you will always remember this.'

He nodded, holding her. She died in his arms, smiling peacefully. He could not remember how long he stayed there with his dead mother in his arms. Next, he heard his father shouting, pulling him away from her and giving him instructions to get his siblings. He was the youngest. He was eight years old.

Relatives and neighbours came, and the funeral was arranged, as is the custom in

Brazil, for the following day. Odecio and his siblings were in shock. No one had explained to them how ill their mother was.

After the funeral, his father gathered the children. In an emotionless tone, chewing some tobacco and spitting on the floor, he told them of his decision. The girls were to be sent to an orphanage and the boys could pack up their bags and fend for themselves on the streets. Odecio's lips started to tremble but he was given a slap and told it was high time that Mummy's little baby grew up.

His father was called Tobias, and he was from Sicily in Italy. There are many rumours about the unscrupulous methods he used to enter and remain in Brazil. Of him I know little. He died before I was born. I only know of his cruelty and total lack of love for his own flesh and blood.

Odecio packed his belongings in a bag and went. He slept rough on park benches. He was traumatised. He had reoccurring dreams about his mother. Her name was Ursula. She was of African descent. Her ancestors were shipped to Brazil from the Portuguese colonies of Angola and Mozambique. She was tall, slim with long limbs. Her skin glowed, it was smooth and the colour of chocolate. She wore her wavy hair up, which gave her a regal air. She had the loveliest smile he had ever seen, with teeth so white they made her entire face light up, just like a full moon light up the sky. She was strict with all her children, kept her home clean and organised with precision. Odecio was immensely proud of her. No one knows how many days, weeks, or months he spent like this, walking alone for miles during the day through the streets of Batatais, sleeping under the stars at night with only his dreams for warmth. His elder brothers all went their separate ways, they were much older and probably had situations into which they could go.

One day he walked so much he found himself out of town, where he spotted a sign:

Help required, apply within

He knocked at the door and a man appeared.

'I am Odecio, and I am enquiring about the job.'

The man laughed and told him to come back in a few more years.

He said to the man, 'I am serious, I will take any job, I don't want any money, just a place to sleep and a plate of food.'

This time the man took him more seriously, called his wife and invited him to lunch. He had never seen a young boy eat so much. Odecio was ravenous. He told them what had happened to him. The wife made the decision for her husband there and then.

'Of course, we need someone just like you to keep the garage clean, wash the tools, make the bookings. I will make a bed for you in the garage. Make sure you fold the mattress and bedclothes each morning and hide it behind the cupboard where the tools are kept.'

He looked at her and for a split second this woman's white face turned dark – her hair turned black, and her smile brightened up the entire kitchen as if the sun had appeared from behind a cloud. He could see Ursula, his mother, smiling with that strict look on her face, telling him to get on with his work.

The work was hard, more and more customers were coming. Odecio started reading about cars, their history, how they were manufactured, how their engines worked. The owner liked Odecio, who was very bright and hard-working. He had never come across anyone, of any age, who felt so happy working. This surprised and delighted the garage owner. He started teaching him the trade. Soon, he was a little mechanic. The only thing he couldn't't do yet was lift the engines out of the cars. Odecio fell in love with the motor car and mechanical engineering. He never seemed interested in money or possessions. The money was just a consequence of his love for his work.

He had never spoken to anyone so candidly about his earlier life. They all listened so intently to him and after he had finished, he noticed that some of them were crying. Chiquinha hugged him gently.

'You are home now, Son, you are home now.'

Iracy fetched him a fresh *cafezinho*. He loved his little cups of strong coffee, but he loved each one of them sitting around that table even more. But he still hated the Church.

So many things were happening:

Odecio was now a Christian, or so everyone thought.

Maria was finally getting married and moving to a rented, tiny, one-bedroom house in Vila Maria.

Iracy was engaged to Odecio, to be married as soon as they had found their house.

Francisca was pre-menopausal and pregnant with her sixteenth child.

The elder siblings were working and almost out of trouble.

The younger siblings were going to school with almost full bellies, proper uniforms, books, and all.

And still no letter, no telegram, not a word from Ana Maria Luisa.

A good woman is hard to find

Maria's wedding took place on a Sunday afternoon at the altar of the Assembly of God. The preacher made sure that the service was extra-long; his sermon went on and on about sinners and their need to repent and serve the Lord. I have a feeling he could smell alcohol on the groom's breath. He had been out the night before with Odecio and some other migrants from the house. The rumour spreading among the guests and the congregation was that the incorrigible Odecio had arranged a wild night for the groom and all the lads.

Finally, he concluded with Corinthians 15.17–20 and pronounced them husband and wife.

'And if Christ be not raised, your faith is vain; ye are yet in your sins. Then they also which are fallen asleep in Christ are perished. If only in this life we have hope in Christ, we are of all men most miserable. But now has Christ rose from the dead and became the first fruits of them that slept.'

Maria looked radiant in her cream-coloured dress with white and blue flowers decorating her long hair. Her groom looked like he always did, distant, with that indifferent bored look on his face, only a bit cleaner, and a touch tidier than usual.

Francisca and Joao were bursting with pride to see their firstborn married. They hid their doubts about the groom. He was now a Christian and in their minds this fact alone exonerated him from his bad and uncaring behaviour towards their daughter.

They moved into a tiny one-bedroom house. There was no honeymoon. Maria had to get up early the next day to go to work. She was now working at a factory, in charge of keeping the toilets clean. She had other jobs in the evening. Her husband could not keep a job for more than a few days. The rent was higher than the bedroom they shared at their previous lodgings, however, Maria wanted more for herself and for her husband: a place of their own with a bit more space and privacy and she desperately wanted a baby. This almost involuntary biological yearning gave her superpowers she did not know she had until then. Nothing fazed her: the long hours at the factory, the piles of dishes and dirty clothes that greeted her every evening when she came home, not even her newly wedded husband, stretched out on the bed, slurring his words.

'There is nothing in this pigsty to eat, Maria.'

She greeted him warmly, sharing all that happened at the factory – the gossip, and the new supervisor, who was an utter pain and knew nothing about keeping toilets clean throughout the day. She tided, she cleaned, she cooked as she talked on and on. She didn't even notice that no one was listening. She was happy, she would feed him, do her best to keep him awake, then she would claim her matrimonial rights. Her baby was on its way; she could feel it in her bones.

She fell pregnant with her first child within just a few months of being married. She was to conceive four children altogether in the years that followed. She remained the breadwinner and had no choice but to leave her children behind in the hands of faith. His drinking got worse. So did the beatings. It would take the greatest loss of her life to finally gather the courage to throw Toninho out for good.

She loves me, she loves me not, she loves me, she loves me not

Odecio was eager to marry. They found a house and he paid the deposit and rent for a year in advance. He was doing well. The house was spacious: two large bedrooms, a lovely living area, a well-equipped kitchen and bathroom, wooden and tiled floors throughout, an outside area for the laundry and barbeques. He let her pick up all the brand-new furniture, curtains, cutlery and crockery. With the help of her mother, she had been getting the *enxoval* ready. The word *enxoval* originates from Arabic, *ax-xawar*, and means the dowry of a marriage. At that time in Brazil this ritual was still practiced. It symbolised the rite of passage of a young single woman living with her parents to an adult married one in charge of her own home. The compilation of the *enxoval* could take years and it consisted of the finest bridal underwear, white sheets, towels and tablecloths of all sizes and shapes for all occasions. This practice finally died out with female emancipation in the seventies.

They had set the date several times, but they would fight over Odecio's drinking or over what he perceived to be her lack of love for him. Neither realised that no amount of love would fill the void left in Odecio's heart. He would forever be that young, rejected orphan walking the streets of Batatais dreaming of his mother. And no amount of pleading from him would melt Iracy's heart, hardened through witnessing too much suffering from such an early age. So, throughout their fifty-four-year marriage, they danced their unique dance, sometimes in step, other times out of step, loving and hating but always deeply caring for each other. They were strong characters, benevolent by nature. They helped many relatives when their worlds collapsed around them. Odecio was a man of his time, conditioned to expect his wife to obey him in a traditional, wifely way. Unfortunately for him, Iracy was a woman well ahead of her time and the ruler of her own heart … and his.

The immaculate conception of two baby boys

It was during that time, when they talked about setting a date for their wedding, that Iracy came home from work one day to find her mother pacing the sitting room floor holding a letter. She handed the letter to Iracy.

'Read it for me, read it now, read it for me please.' They were both frozen on the spot, staring at each other. Time stood still for both. Iracy opened the letter.

My darling dearest Mamae,

I know I don't deserve your love. It has taken me so long to write, to send you news. I am a selfish inconsiderate daughter.

But I am a bearer of good news. I have been travelling a lot with the funfair company. The work is hard, but the pay is good and I love it when the lights go on and the people start to arrive. He has been so good to me. He is a caring, romantic man and lets me know how much he loves me every day.

I am now with his child. We are thrilled with the news, though he does not think it possible to love this child like he loves me, Mother. I tell him I have enough love in my heart for them both.

I am now seven months pregnant. I had a scare, a bit of bleeding. He has taken me to the doctors who recommended rest. Nonsense I told him. But my husband (yes, we are married Mamae) insists that I stay put and stop travelling. So, when the fair leaves this town in a week or so, I shall be staying behind. We rented a lovely house with some land and some chickens.

I hope you can forgive me and come to visit me. I will be so alone here in the wilderness. He will be back in less than a month for the birth.

I've got an address now, please get Iracy to write me all the news. I want to know how everyone is. Tell her I want minuscule details about everyone and everything and juicy gossip too.

All my love

Your selfish inconsiderate travelling Ana Maria Luisa.

Iracy had no words, she just hugged her tiny, pregnant mum and let her cry.

Iracy slept badly. Her intuition was telling her that something needed to be done fast. Her pregnant, impulsive sister could not be trusted to rest. She had already had a scare.

In the morning she shared her worries with her mother. She convinced her parents to go and stay with Ana Maria Luisa to make sure she rested. This was also an opportunity for her mum and dad to take a break. She would take them over there at the weekend.

She shared the news with Odecio, who insisted he got a car to take them all there on Saturday.

Odecio and Joao watched, feeling a mixture of amusement and concern, as the daughters and bumps engulfed each other in one endless hug. They cried, they screamed, they jumped in unison, laughing at being reunited after such a long time.

The weekend was spent cooking, eating, eating and cooking some more. Sharing stories over endless *cafezinhos*. Thousands of words flying gently rapidly from eager mouths. So much to share in just forty-eight hours.

Time flies when there is not enough time to share all the events of the past few years and soon it was time to go. Iracy left a number where she could be easily contacted, just in case they needed anything. With a mind full of apprehension, she left her sister and her parents in a strange house, in a strange town.

On the way back, Iracy told Odecio she had never been more certain that they should marry as soon as possible. Bursting with happiness, he gave her hand a tiny squeeze. Little did they know that the events about to follow would burst their bubble.

A few days later, Iracy received a call at work from her mother, who had managed to find the local bakery to make the call. Ana Maria Luisa had another scare and was taken to the local medical centre. They had no way of contacting her husband. Her mum's blood pressure was dangerously high.

Iracy arrived alone, in no time at all, to find her sister lying in a hospital bed. Taking one look at her sister she immediately sensed her despair, she seemed like that lost waif of a girl, with a runny nose and a head full of lice, all over again.

'Stay calm, Ana Maria Luisa, stay strong. The doctor told me the baby is coming early, but he said not to worry, at seven months he stands a good chance of surviving. His little heartbeat is mighty strong.'

'Iracy, promise me you will take care of my baby if I don't make it. I asked God to take me. I have had a good life, I have known passion, adventure. I have chosen to give this baby my life if it comes to it.'

'Stop talking like this, both of you will be fine.'

But Ana Maria Luisa heard the lack of conviction in her intuitive sister's voice. She always thought of Iracy as a psychic Tupi-Guarani witch.

At 3am, after a very painful birth, little Gilberto was born, all wrinkled up, two months premature but with a powerful set of lungs. Both sisters laughed. He was a tough little fighter that one!

Iracy placed little Gilberto in his mother's arms. He lay there already searching for her breast, for his sustenance, being gently stroked by his beautiful, pale, and serene mother. She lifted her eyes, smiling at her sister. She looked radiant.

'I never thought it would be possible to feel this unbelievable amount of love again, Iracy. Only this is pure, divine. If there is a heaven, it must feel like this.'

She cradled her baby in her arms, giving him her breast. She looked up to Iracy.

'This is cracking my heart right open. It feels as if I am melting into this little creature; I don't want to be anywhere else but here.'

At 5am Luisa started to hemorrhage. The local hospital had neither the equipment nor the expertise to stop it. There was also a shortage of ambulances.

Ana Maria Luisa could not be transported to a bigger hospital and died at 8am of a post-partum hemorrhage. She was nineteen years old.

She was buried in a strange cemetery, in that strange little town, with a strange precarious medical centre.

Iracy spent the next few weeks nursing Gilberto and her mum, who had become ill with grief, and consoling her father who had stopped speaking, eating, sleeping, and functioning.

She called for Odecio. In no time at all he was there with breads, meats, fresh coffee, posh little cakes, nappies, formula milk, brand-new blue baby grows, blue mittens, blue hats and a suitcase filled with baby clothes donated by the members of the Assembly of God. He also carried with him a heart full of sadness.

Odecio tried to make enquiries about the funfair company to no avail. They decided to stay and wait for baby Gilberto's father to return.

Three weeks went by and eventually they heard someone coming up the path. His steps were quick and purposeful. They could hear him humming a little nursery rhyme; he was carrying his case in one hand and a huge bunch of flowers in the other.

Iracy's heart missed a bit and she hurried to greet him at the door.

'Hi, I am Luisa's sister, Iracy, it is good to meet you, I am here with my mum and dad. We came to help her, there have been some complications.' Opening the door ajar, he walked right past her.

'Luisa, Ana Maria Luisa, I am here now!'

Mauricio walked fast from room to room, he saw Joao Inacio and Francisca looking forlorn and sitting on the marital bed. Not so long ago, he laid in that very same bed, spooning Luisa, caressing her swollen belly, rubbing her back, doing all he could to make her comfortable. She was everything to him. They shared a passion for each other that increased the more he delved into her mysteries. She knew just how to ignite his passion; she knew how to soothe him when he was feeling low. And she made him laugh, she was outrageously funny, cared little about what others thought about her. She was alive, curious, passionate from the moment she woke up to the moment when her head finally touched her pillow after a long back-breaking day. She had time and compassion for everyone. However, very few were brave enough to cross her. She had a fierce temper and knew how to throw a punch better than any man. Life in her presence was unpredictable and exciting.

I guess that leaving her family behind to follow Mauricio, and work and travel with the funfair meant that Ana Maria Luisa had freed herself from her parent's expectations, from the rigid doctrine of their new religion. It had also freed her from the grueling existence poor migrants had to endure to survive in the city. Finding herself cut loose, her true passionate nature had the chance to blossom.

Mauricio walked to the second bedroom, spotting his tiny son asleep in the cot. He turned to Iracy, who was right behind him. 'Where is she?' he screamed, 'Where is she?'

Iracy held his arm firmly, asking him to sit down.

'First tell me, where is she? Where is my Luisa?'

'I am so sorry. She hemorrhaged a few hours after the birth. They didn't have the right equipment, the right doctors, an ambulance even. They tried, they really did, please calm down, meet your son, he is a little fighter, born two months premature.'

He stopped, looking lost in his own Kafka's nightmare, walked over to the crib, and picked up his son. He started to shake the baby and scream.

'You killed her, you killed her, why did you have to come early, who told you to come early? You were supposed to wait for me, you killed her.'

It took all of Iracy's strength and powers of persuasion to get little Gilberto back. She took the baby while her mum and dad tried to console their broken son-in-law, whom they had just met.

Not another word was said. He picked up his unpacked suitcase and the flowers, and asked where she was buried. They all walked with him to the cemetery. He laid the flowers on her grave and without another word he left, never to be seen again.

Iracy spent the next few days nursing the baby, helping her mother to regain her strength. Francisca cried, prayed, and read the Bible.

My grandmother had acquired a brand-new empty hole in her heart, filled by the vibrant red lipstick lips, eager eyes, dazzling dresses, girly giggle ghost of her daughter – a dead young mother.

There was never a trace of a single tear in Iracy's eyes. Instead, she had that mad look on her face, which meant she was plotting her next move.

She told Odecio the wedding was off.

'What about the house?'

'Only the wedding is off Odecio. I need the house. I am moving in with *Mamae*, *Papai* and the baby. They need me; the others are capable now of paying the rent on my parents' house keeping things ticking for a while. *Mamae* needs rest and stability for a while. She is due in just a month.'

He did not argue. He did as he was told. He never questioned her decisions again; he would follow her to the ends of the earth.

Her baby brother, Carlos, was born at a healthy weight. Although he was delivered without any complications, Francisca stayed in hospital for some time, for the doctors could not find what was wrong with her: their comprehensive training at medical school had not given them the tools do deal with that amount of grief.

> *eight ghosts*
> *stayed with her*
> *trying forever to fill*
> *eight empty holes in a tiny mother's*
heart

So Iracy and Odecio became surrogate parents to two very demanding bouncing baby boys. They cared for them with diligence, tenacity, and a lot of love. Iracy was twenty-one years of age, Odecio was twenty-five.

They used to go out with the boys, feeling very proud of how they were growing into healthy happy toddlers. Iracy was often called ugly names by those who did not know the story.

'There goes that whore, single mother of two with her fancy pimp by her side.'

She would look them in the eye and say, 'Yes, I am the mother of these little boys, but I am not a whore. It was an immaculate conception; you see in front of you two brand-new baby Jesuses. The world got so bad with badmouth cruel pricks like you around that our Lord sent two this time. So be careful what you say.'

Odecio would run after them ready for a fight. Afterwards they would relive that moment and laugh aloud together. They laughed a lot together. Carlos and Gilbert would join in without getting the jokes and the four of them would cry with laughter.

Two years went by; Francisca was much stronger. One Sunday afternoon, when the toddlers were having their afternoon naps, she called Iracy and Odecio and sat them down.

'You two have done more, so much more, went beyond the call of duty to help us all. It is time you got married. Orminda and Lourdes are soon to be married, Sebastiao, Espedito, and even young Messias are already courting young women from the church. Soon it will be only Onofre left to marry. I will have the space to take care of the boys. Your dad can no longer take the brutal schedule of the building sites, he bought a sweet trolley to sell at the schools and funfairs, Onofre is on a good wage. It is not healthy for them to think you are their *mamae* and *papai*. It is not fair on you not to be making your life together, having your own children. It is time now.'

Who could argue with that?

Odecio was proud of his achievements. From nothing, he had trained as an excellent mechanic, his business was growing, and he had his bride. Not to mention how his hunger for knowledge and his preoccupation with world affairs had turned him into a well-read self-educated little orphan. He decided to take Iracy to meet his father. Let bygones be bygones. He was an adult now.

They arrived in Batatais, on a bright, sunny day, dressed in their Sunday best. The house he was forced to leave looked old, dirty and uncared for. Inside, the curtains were shut, sunlight was fighting to be let in, making strange shadows on the walls of the gloomy rooms. It smelt of damp and hospitals. Odecio's heart was pounding, he felt eight years of age all over again. Time had stood still in that house. He wanted to leave and run away. He should never have come back.

They walked into the lounge where old Tobias was sitting. It had been a few decades since he threw his youngest into the streets.

He got up and looked at them both. Odecio was so nervous, trying hard to deal with the rollercoaster of emotions engulfing him. He went into verbal overdrive, talking fast, trying to fill the awkward silence in the dark room.

'Hi Pai, as you probably heard, I am doing well, I am a car mechanic now, there is nothing I don't know about the motor engine. My business is doing well. I am getting married next month, Pai, and here she is!'

Filled with pride he turned to Iracy to introduce her, 'I came here to show her off,' said Odecio, trying to add some light humour to that stifling situation.

Tobias looked at Iracy up and down and down and up, with a cold indifference that sent shivers down her spine.

'Now you have. I am off fishing. See yourselves out.'

'Yes, let's get out of this damp, Odecio,' Iracy said, holding his arm a little tighter. 'You have a real family now.'

Consumed with rage, with murderous thoughts in her head, she gave old Tobias one of her evil looks, spat on the floor and took her groom away with her.

The wedding invitation remained all crumpled up in the inner pocket of Odecio's best jacket.

I feel that the circumstances of his early life, the loss of his mother and the cold heartiness of his father and elder siblings, left inside my father a black hole of such magnitude that anything, however insignificant or irrelevant, would trigger feelings of abandonment. When this happened, he would revert to being that lost little boy again, he could not control the hurt he felt, and anger would take over. Following his unreasonable outbursts of rage, fueled by alcohol, he would fall into a state of deep sorrow. I for one, could not bear to see him in such emotional chaos. For as long as I can remember, I would try and reach out to him.

'Come on, *Papai*, it is all ok now, get up, go wash and get ready for bed, you got work tomorrow.'

He, like a child, on hearing the worry and affection in my voice, would do as he was told. He never missed a day's work; he never took any holidays but money in lieu and at weekends he would often take on more jobs. Later in life he would develop severe sleeping problems. Due to his tenacity and love for his work, he managed to keep a roof over our heads and our bellies full.

Years later, when Odecio received news that his father was dying, without uttering a single word, he went back to fixing his cars whilst whistling a song that was being played on the radio. He did not go to the funeral. He never mentioned his father again.

Iracy looked spendid in her white satin wedding dress that suited her slim figure. A wide, fashionable matching hat completed her bridal outfit; the white satin made her dark complexion and dark eyes stand out; she looked tiny and so young for her age. Odecio was dashing in his dark suit, shiny shoes, and black wavy hair with just a curl falling on his forehead. He looked like he always did. Impossible to improve on perfection.

Iracy felt a bit uneasy as she made her way down the aisle. She wondered what her life would be like as a married woman, especially as a woman married to Odecio. So far, she had been the driver and the executer of her decisions, the uncertainty of how her life with Odecio would turn out made her a bit on edge. However, when she saw her groom standing at the altar, looking dashingly handsome and as lost as she felt, she could not imagine herself being married to anyone else. She spotted her mother, father, brothers, and sisters all smiling at her and she no longer felt alone; she remembered her mother's tales of her own union to her father when she was barely thirteen and how her grandmother and great aunties were a constant source of support to young Francisca. These thoughts helped her feel that she was doing the right thing and her last remaining steps towards Odecio were filled with a determined excitement.

The church was decorated with lovely fresh flowers. It was packed with family, friends, and curious members of the Assembly of God. Odecio and Iracy were a very unusual and vibrant couple with so many stories to tell.

They were followed by two pageboys; uncle Carlos, aged three – Francisca's last child – and his nephew Gilberto – Ana Maria Luisa's son also aged three, dressed in little white suits, frilly blue shirts, carrying one wedding ring each. They looked adorable. But they cried throughout the ceremony, with Gilberto making incomprehensible sounds that only Iracy could understand as only a mother can make sense of her child's cries.

'*Maezinha*, please don't leave me.'

At three years of age little Gilberto could not have imagined that Iracy would forever be his fairy Godmother; like the time when she orchestrated a cunning plan to help him escape the young offenders prison he found himself in a decade or so later. It transpired that young Gilberto had been committing petty crimes and small burglaries on the streets of São Paulo. One day his luck ran out and he was detained in a tough young offender's unit outside of the city. News travelled fast in the Vila Maria grapevine: when hearing that her nephew – also her son in so many ways – was in deep trouble, she went to his rescue. She went to visit him immediately. She found him traumatised, in shock and beaten up by the mindless sadists they put in charge of those

116

offending boys. She opened her arms to hug him, but he avoided her and silently stared at the floor. She became aware that he was beyond reach. She asked him to show her around the grounds: they walked past fields fenced off with barbed wire. She noticed a small stream covered by vegetation and trees. She asked him to sit on the grass by the stream. She instructed him to look at the stream and the fence. They stared and stared at the stream and at the fence in silence while the wardens walked up and down supervising the visits. She then instructed Gilberto to dig under the fence until there was enough space for him to crawl under, telling him to work calmly, with great care and focus a little every day, never forgetting to cover the hole with leaves and twigs or allow anyone to see him. She gave him the Bible and he used it as alibi while sitting by the stream. She said she would visit at the same time each week. Each week they sat by the stream reading the Bible. During one of her visits, she asked him if he was ready and he nodded.

She said, 'When they let you out to the bathrooms at night, make a run to the stream and swim over the other side, a car will be there to collect you.'

She went home. She told Odecio to fetch a good car from one of his clients and be ready for 7.30 pm.

'We are going on an adventure, Odecio, just the two of us,' she said, being sweet and seductive.

At 7.15 pm, Odecio picked her up excitedly, ready for the adventure. They set out in the borrowed car. She instructed him to drive. Slowly she revealed her wicked plan to rescue her nephew.

'You what? Have you gone insane? This could end with all of us in jail!'

'You helped me rescue him once and you are going to do it again. Otherwise on your head be it when he is beaten or abused to death by those animals in charge or turns into a hardened criminal if he manages to get out alive.'

And who could argue with that? The plan was executed without a flaw. When they arrived, he ran to the car, a shadow of the healthy, high-spirited boy he had been before he went in. He stank of the sewage from the toxic little stream. Iracy instructed him to lie on the floor of the car, covered him with a blanket and gave him a Tupperware box filled with food, a bottle of sugared water to calm him down and a very thick slice of *fuba* cake.

She had even planned different safe places where he would stay, moving from house to house, keeping a low profile, living out of a rucksack, never leaving behind any trace of his presence.

Before she sent him on his way, fed, watered, clean and smelling human again, they hugged, and he sobbed for a long time.

'*Maezinha*, please don't leave me.'

'I won't be doing this again for you, Gilberto. Keep your head high, your nose clean and in a few years there will be no records of you ever being detained. In the meantime, find yourself any kind of work you can get. Odecio was also an orphan with no one at all to look out for him, but he never stole an apple from anyone. You can do this. But if you go back to the streets, eventually you will be dead or back in prison. It is a choice that only you can make. The easy option is often the hardest in the long run, I hope you can see that now. I hope you have learned your lesson. Now go, I will be in touch when it is safe!'

In the years to come Gilberto fell in and out of trouble but not the kind of trouble that landed one in prison or shot dead on the streets of São Paulo. Eventually he would settle down. He went to work as a private chauffeur for one of the richest men in South America. He married, had children, grandchildren and even became a great-grandfather. Making Iracy an immensely proud great-great-grand auntie. In fact, a great-great-grandmother – *Tataravo*.

A lifetime would go by, like the turn of a page, until Gilberto would beg for her to stay again. My mum was convalescing after the first cruel stroke that left her partially blind. She was eighty-two years old. Gilberto came to visit, and I found him kneeling by her bed, whimpering like a baby.

'*Maezinha*, (little mummy), please be strong, please get better, don't leave me.'

Maria and her two girls

From my Auntie Maria I inherited the ability to cry and to laugh very easily. I also learnt the importance of taking pride in the work you do, no matter what it is. This work ethic came in handy for me as I did all sorts of jobs while studying in England. My memories of her are imprinted in the core of my being. She worked for many years at a factory cleaning toilets. She smelt of bleach. She would stop by on her way home. I still love the smell of bleach. She was a great cook and a creative cake maker. She made all the cakes for all the weddings, christenings and birthdays for family and friends. She never charged a penny.

I always wondered why she did not value her skills as a brilliant baker; why could she not have been a bit more entrepreneurial, left the factory and set up her own little business. I have a feeling that even before the age of five, she took on the subservient role that was assigned to her; her duty as the eldest was to be useful to her constantly pregnant and sick mother. She could not see her potential or her worth.

On the day of her retirement, she stopped at our house.

'*Tia* Maria, it is your last day at work. At last! Are you happy?' I asked her, I was really excited for her.

'No, I loved working at the factory, in charge of keeping the toilets clean. The factory girls would come in, tell me all their troubles, I would listen carefully and try and find some pearls of wisdom but mostly they just needed a shoulder to cry on or a fresh handkerchief. I always made sure the toilets were spotless for them when they came in during their breaks or when they left work.'

And she cried as she always did when she opened her heart to speak her truth, and I cried with her too, not sure why.

That stayed with me forever. To my Auntie Maria it was not important what job she did if she felt she served a purpose for someone.

On the many occasions when Iracy and Odecio fell out after their endless fights, and the little orphan that lived inside my father could no longer bear to be treated like a dog in his own house, by the hard-hearted little girl that lived inside my mother, he would pack a few of his things, threatening to leave her forever. He hung around hoping she would say three little words, 'please don't go,' but instead she simply said, 'that is the door', and he would walk a few miles to Maria's house.

She would make him a *cafezinho*, and listen without saying a word to his lamentations about her evil sister; seeing him in such despair pulled at her heartstrings and she would ask him tearfully,

'What will you do, Odecio? You are just as bad; you were made for each other.' And he would return with his tail between his legs. Iracy would laugh, we would all laugh. When he laughed, we knew everything would be fine until the next time.

When my father was ill after an operation, unable to work, struggling to feed his family, the sight of Maria arriving at our house with bags of groceries and homemade soups for him will always be one of my happiest childhood memories. Iracy would unpack the groceries, digging for the maize flour, sugar, eggs, milk, and butter to bake her *fuba* cake. Odecio would dig into the grocery bag for the fresh coffee to make a brew. Together, they would share the *fuba* cake, the strong *cafezinhos*, stories about family members and juicy gossip of the secret sins committed by some despicable members of the Assembly of God; Odecio would make some outrageously funny and filthy remarks about everyone, and they would laugh like children. At times like these, I thought my young heart would burst with love and pride for the three of them. They seemed so alone against this big bad world that denied them their basic human rights, yet they exuded confidence, strength, hope, humour, and humanity.

Despite her disastrous union with Toninho, Maria had two children: one boy and a girl. She adored her children. Motherhood can give some women, even in unfavourable

123

circumstances, an extra reservoir of energy and hope. This was the case with her. She worked hard, managed her flawed relationship with her husband and tried to create the best environment she could for her children.

What motherhood could not give Maria were supernatural powers when she needed them most.

Maria Emilia was twenty months old when she fell ill. What had started as a minor cold and fever became worrying when Maria came home from work to find that her temperature had gone up and she was not taking any food or water. Toninho oversaw the children when Maria was at work with the help of a kind neighbour or young relative willing to give a hand.

They lived in one of the many ghettos that had sprung up all over São Paulo to house the ever-growing influx of migrants from all over Brazil. They were small dwellings with a basic kitchen and a large room; an outside bathroom was shared with other families. The large room was divided by a makeshift curtain to create a division between sleeping and sitting areas.

'Toninho, we must take her to a hospital now.'

'You are always fussing over these kids, give it a break, will you?' She noticed that he had been drinking. There was no point in engaging with him.

She picked up the child and managed to find someone to take her to the hospital. At this point she knew her baby girl had much more wrong with her than a strong bout of flu. She held her close all the way in the back of the car. She prayed with all her might; she sang hymns to the child. She had a deep certainty in her heart that Jesus would not take her child away from her.

The doctors could not save Maria Emilia. Her meningitis was too advanced. She died that night in hospital.

The death of a child brings unbelievable despair to a parent, a pain so great that not many can face it and survive with sufficient courage to face the world again: such loss will transform a parent forever. Maria could not accept the desolating finality of Maria Emilia's death. A hatred for Toninho started to corrode her mind, her heart, the core of her being. On the way back from the hospital she had made up her mind; she would tolerate him until she was with child again, before throwing him out and eradicating him from her life forever. This thought gave her strength.

She went to church twice a week now. Iracy and Odecio did all they could to console her. She was worrying them. She was delusional and convinced that she was going to conceive her daughter again. That God was sending her back. She promised God she would protect her this time with her own life.

She soon became pregnant. Throughout her pregnancy she was convinced that her Maria Emilia was coming back to her. Unknown to her, and everyone around her, Maria was having a psychotic break – where the mind can only cope by distorting reality and creating a new reality where one is able to protect the psyche from disintegration.

Soon her new baby was born with a strong heartbeat and a powerful pair of lungs. The baby looked remarkably like Maria Emilia: the same light-olive skin, dark eyes, volumes of shiny black hair, the same well-defined arched eyebrows, the same round face, and cupid bow's little mouth. The only difference was that this baby was a boy.

Maria did not feel sadness or joy on his arrival. She became empty, hollow-eyed, distant, disassociated from everyday living. She called him Fabio.

Iracy would visit often to take care of her sister and the boys. One day she arrived unexpectedly.

'Maria, I think it would be healthy if we went through Maria Emilia's things, she has been gone for a while now. I have brought some new little pieces for Fabio.'

Iracy walked to the baby's cot to change him and to her horror, she noticed the baby was dressed in a pink frilly dress, little pink socks, and white shoes; decorating his head were two of Maria Emilia's white and pink hair bows. He was dressed in what once was Maria

Emilia's christening outfit. For a split second she saw her dead little niece, the resemblance was frightening. Iracy picked her nephew up, changed him into his new blue sailor outfit, and handed him over to Maria.

As she held her baby boy, silent tears started to fall, one by one wetting Fabio's little face.

'I don't dress him like this every day, I don't, Iracy, you've got to believe me, it is the only way I can cope some days.'

'You are hurting, I cannot begin to imagine how much. Be careful, you are still so bereaved, I fear for your mind, for little Fabio. Please be careful, don't let anyone see this.'

I don't know how long this went on for, the sisters kept their secret for an entire lifetime. When my mum had her first stroke, I nursed her for a few weeks. During that time, she had a need to talk about her now-deceased sister. It was the first time she had shared their secret with anyone. I feel that carrying the enormity of this secret was weighing her down. She felt guilty for not being able to help her sister. She felt guilty for going along with that macabre situation.

Maria had another child with Toninho, still hoping for a girl. She had another boy. By then her bereavement and delusional behaviour was under control and Fabio was no longer a baby.

At that time in Brazil little was known about transgenderism. By the time Fabio was three it was clear to everyone that he had a strong female psyche; both his mannerisms and the way he spoke were ultra-feminine. He preferred dolls and liked to wear little dresses and jewellery.

Maria kept her promise to herself and eradicated Toninho from her life. News arrived years later that he had died alone of liver failure. He was buried in a paupers' pit. Maria felt nothing, said nothing, not a word was mentioned to her sons.

She still worked hard to keep the boys and they were left to their own devices, soon running with other kids through the narrow, crowded lanes of their ghetto.

By the age of twelve, Fabio had developed an androgynous look: long hair, painted toenails, tight bell-bottoms, and bell-sleeve blouses tied with a knot above his ribcage revealing his smooth, light-brown navel. He wore very subtle make-up – just a bit of black eyeliner and a touch of lip gloss. He was a beautiful, exotic creature. He was gregarious, creative, fun, and a great dancer. To this day, his image to me symbolises the epitome of glamour and body confidence.

But it was the early 1960s in São Paulo, Brazil. Fabio evoked anger and disgust, and even secret lust in some of the males in the family. While Maria worked, his uncles took it upon themselves to fix him. The beatings were relentless, justified by their good intentions to help the boy turn into a proper man.

One of the last acts of physical and psychological abuse against Fabio, always camouflaged by the good intention of helping Maria, came when my father and other uncles spread a strong type of industrial glue on his entire head while he slept. To this day I have an intuition that my cousin was never asleep while this was going on but paralysed with fear.

When the culprits returned to our house, Iracy noticed that something was wrong by their hushed voices and sheepish manner.

'What have you done to him now?' Her voice was quiet, but you could hear the anger and disgust she felt for them.

'We are doing what we think is right by him. Protecting him the way you do is making matters worse, giving him permission to be perverted.'

'What have you done to him?' She was screaming at the top of her voice. 'If anything happens to him you will regret the day you were born. I will make you all pay for your brutality, your unkindness, your self-righteousness. And call Maria at the factory now, ask her to come home.'

When she got to her sister's house he was there, quietly shivering all over in his bed, which was now too small for him. Iracy sat by his bed.

'Listen to me – I need you to take a few deep breaths, I am here now. Your mum will be here soon. I promise you that I will do everything in my power for all of this to stop once and for all. You are in shock, but I am here now, and I am taking you to the hospital for them to fix you up, then we are going to the police.'

Maria soon arrived smelling of bleach, red-eyed, broken-spirited, in shock.

Fabio was hospitalised for a couple of nights. They did the best they could. In time the wounds left on his scalp healed, the ones inflicted in his heart could never heal.

The sisters managed to put a restraining order on the culprits. No charges were pressed. The police turned a blind eye to the mountain of domestic issues they witnessed every day. Some prominent officers secretly approved of what they called 'queer bashing.' This goes on to this day in certain parts of Brazil.

Iracy kept a closer eye on her nephew; when my father was at work, he would spend time with us. Soon his hair, alongside his courage grew. I used to love his visits, I would stare at his latest look, his latest fashion creations, his beauty, his zest for life. His presence brightened my days.

'Kirinha, have you heard this song? It is called the twist, it is from America.'

'Never heard of it!'

'Well, there is a new dance for this song.' He would grab me by the hand. 'Let's twist again, like we did last summer, Ohhh, let's twist again, la la la.' Off he went, making sounds that sounded like English, 'Now,

Kirinha, twist your heels back and forth – swish swish swish – now move your elbows in the same direction, twist your body from side to side, and now the difficult part, all the way down, twisting all the way down.'

He was a brilliant dancer, twisting and turning his body in harmony with the song's beat in a perfect effortless flow, unlike me, who looked like a total idiot, red in the face from too much effort. He did it with joy, he did it sensually. He inspired me to move and conduct myself as a woman more than any other female in the family!

Soon after the hair incident, Maria moved with the three boys to my grandmother's house. Most of her siblings had married and moved away. It was under my grandparents' roof that Fabio was groomed and abused by an uncle and later by another distant relative.

Before his fifteenth birthday he left his family behind. He found new friends and a brand-new family where he was accepted. He found his tribe. Maria, Iracy and I used to visit him at his lodgings in the centre of São Paulo where he lived with kindred spirits. Our visits were kept secret.

He and his new friends did what they could to earn a living and escape the brutality of their so-called loved ones. As a young adult, Fabio created a one-man show that was accepted at a renowned theatre in São Paulo. He described it to me as a powerful healing experience. He designed an outfit whereby the left side was a traditional male suit and the other half a glamorous, long emerald-green evening gown with sequins and a split on the side; the show would start with him sitting in the middle of the stage in total darkness while the uplifting sound of Vivaldi's 'Spring' filled the theatre as the audience took to their seats. Then the music would slowly fade, the lights on the stage would first light the male side of his body; Fabio would engage the audience, sharing episodes of his life as a boy, detailing them with passion and humour. Then the chair would turn around to reveal him dressed as a glamorous young woman.

'This woman you now see in front of you,' he would say to the audience and pause for almost a minute allowing the audience to digest his transformation, 'this may shock and disgust you, but she is the one who lives inside my male body. She is my essence, my mind, my heart, and my soul.'

The show ran for a year or more and received glowing reviews. The approval he received from the strangers in the audience healed him. It freed him to be who he really was.

Years later, he paid everyone an unexpected visit to my grandma's birthday party. He arrived sporting an outrageously androgynous look. He was wearing a tasteful jumpsuit in black with tiny specks of Yves Saint Laurent blue, black toenails poking out of high-heeled leather sandals, perfectly French-manicured long, fingernails, subtle make-up enhancing his beautiful features and long hair so shiny and glossy that made us girls feel envious, self-conscious, and totally uncool. He was training to be a hairdresser. By his side was his lover: a six-foot-tall broad-shouldered Black God. There was no way his tiny uncles could get past this giant of a man who loved Fabio and was there to protect him. The subtlety of that unspoken revenge felt ever so sweet.

He continued to visit his mother and Iracy. There was no longer anything to fear; he was free to visit us even if the men of the house would walk out as soon as he arrived. We did not care about that and enjoyed catching up with him.

After some years living in the centre of São Paulo, he went to Paris and lived there for a few decades. He had transgendered and now lived as a woman. She met the love of her life, and they were happy for many years until she was forced to return to Brazil when the French immigration officials denied her the right to remain in Paris.

Fabio now went by the name of Francoise La Dulce. Francoise returned to São Paulo, worked as a hairdresser, and took care of her mother. While Maria made the cakes for all the weddings, christenings and birthdays for the entire family, Francoise was our gorgeous, talented personal hairdresser, make-up artist and French teacher.

We took no notice of the fact that whenever she entered a house, all the men would get up and leave. Years later, during one of my visits, Francoise came to my mum's house to meet my husband. Paul was shocked and saddened to witness the men's discomfort and how they all made a quick exit through the back door. Paul and Francoise, with my help as translator, get on like a house on fire. Times were slowly changing.

As two adult women we talked about her journey and transformation into a transgender woman. We also talked about the brutality young Fabio went through. Francoise shared with me that she had seen several psychiatrists who helped her come to terms with her gender identity. The years of therapy also helped her find forgiveness. She expressed that had she not found forgiveness, her mind would be forever trapped in the abuse she endured as a young boy.

She shared with me a reoccurring dream. She took great comfort in this dream. Sometimes in her dream she was born a little girl, she saw the girl growing up into a young woman, having children and walking arm in arm with her mother Maria while they both watched her children play. Sometimes she was the mother and Maria her little girl whom she fiercely protected with her own life. In her reoccurring dream, she was serene, happy, and so was Maria.

When my father was dying, calling for my brother to bring him his dentures – Odecio was vain and took care of his immaculate appearance to the very end, he did not want anyone criticising the appearance of his corpse as he laid in his coffin – it was Francoise who came to his rescue, got the dentures and put them in for him, combing his hair and smoothing his brow.

'Now Uncle, you are all fixed up. Dentures are in, perfect hair, you look beautiful, you can relax now,' and she softly kissed his forehead.

She taught me the greatest lesson in forgiveness.

> There is no need for temples, no need for complicated philosophies, my mind and my heart are my temples, and my philosophy is kindness.
>
> The Dalai Lama

As soon as Iracy and Odecio were married, they left the Assembly of God and its oppressive ways. The blind faith of its members, who could not see the hypocrisy of their more unscrupulous followers, had become intolerable to them.

Iracy became the black sheep of the family. Francisca was devastated to see her daughter give up on Christ.

'*Mamae*, I am not giving up on any of his teachings, I am not. I don't need to go to church to practice what I know is in his heart. I don't think he said that all we need to do is to turn up in church, hear the sermons, sing a few hymns, and put nothing into practice, I am sure that's not what he meant at all.'

'Iracy, the world is full of sinners, if you do not belong to the Church, you will be associating yourself with them.'

'*Mamae*, we are just humans, we are not meant to be perfect, we are not saints or sinners. To me it is not that simple. People are complex. What life does to them can really dictate their actions. Some are stronger, some are weaker, some are eviler than others. And as for sin, I am not sure what that means; think about it, if a hungry child steals a piece of bread, is he a sinner or just famished? Is it right to believe in a God who will only take the believers to heaven, leaving the rest to perish? Would you, as a mother, save some of your children and leave the others to burn in hell? I see things so very differently now, *Mamae*. If there is a God, he gave us life and to me life is rare, it is a miracle and we owe it to him to have the best lives we can but with joy, with purpose not with misery and guilt. We are what we are and yes, there is hurt here made by us but there is also so much beauty too. Just look around you, Creation is everywhere, in the trees, in the flowers, in your grandchildren's laughter, in you who is so wise and kind despite all you have gone through; you are my little miraculous *Mamae*.

'I am tired Ma, so tired of the Church, there is no joy for me there, just obligation. It infuriates me to see a lot of the church members exercising a sense of superiority over the rest of us. Where is the compassion? Where is the kindness for the human plight?'

Francisca had no answers for her daughter, she just shook her head and stayed quiet, lost in her incomprehensible thoughts. Iracy felt guilty to have shared with her mother how she truly felt and how she was changing; how she was beginning to challenge and reassess everything she had been taught so far. She had adopted a habit of sitting for extended periods of time in deep reflection. This practice would give her, at crucial times in her life, an absolute clarity of what action to take and the ability to filter out what felt untruthful to her; these reflective moments connected her even more deeply with her intuition and with that unexplainable force that guided her throughout her life. She became increasingly courageous, living life by her own rules, doing what she felt was right for herself and protecting those she loved. In doing so, she liberated me in so many ways from a patriarchal society full of hypocritical values that devalued women. She showed me my own worth. She gave me the courage to live by my own rules, she showed me what was needed to survive in a world made by rules that only benefited a few.

'Can I still visit you and everyone, *Mamae*?'

'I told you before, wherever I am will always be your home.' Francisca looked closely at her rebellious daughter, 'You look so much like my mother, Iracy, you have inherited not only her Tupi-Guarani genes but also her unfathomable spirit.'

The matter was settled. But she was always criticised in hushed tones for leaving the Church, for speaking the unspeakable, for the way she brought up her children, for her unkempt house, for defying her husband, for laughing too loud, for breaking the rules, for her new hair style, for her painted red lips. And they prayed for her without noticing that she was the one to pick up the pieces when someone in the family was in trouble. They failed to see that although her house was a bit of a mess, she had ample time to be with her children, to listen to them, to read them stories and even time to rescue her nephews, to listen to and advise her nieces and her cousin's daughters when they got into trouble and could not go home to their own mothers. Yes, they failed to see all of that: they failed to see the true Christian among them.

Despite having no idea who the Dalai Lama was, Iracy's heart was her temple, and her practicing philosophy was kindness. Throughout her life she helped many relatives – housing, feeding, and comforting them. In her later years, she became extremely conversant with the complex and bureaucratic nature of the Brazilian national health service. She assisted countless illiterate relatives and neighbours to navigate these services and get the treatments they needed. She fought hard for their rights to free and humane healthcare.

There are many acts of kindness that Iracy carried out throughout her life. Too many to be mentioned here; there were also instances when she acted out of her own interests with no consideration for others. She was no saint; she was a strong-willed woman. Her survival and the survival of her loved ones were much more important than some inexplicable rules that had the tendency to crush those who, out of fear, insisted on following them.

Her darkness was especially visible in her treatment of her daughters-in-law. I am sure these women have many stories they can share on this topic. She was a matriarchal powerhouse and the presence of other females encroaching on her territory and getting all the attention from her boys must have aroused in her feelings of insecurity and a jealously, which she tried to hide, especially from herself. But she also knew her elder sons and how vulnerable they had become due to their own childhood traumas, their life choices, and addictions. She spent the rest of her life trying to protect them from themselves. When she thought she was going to die, her main concern was still for them.

However, I witnessed her darkness far less often than I witnessed her unmeasurable force when there was someone who needed help.

It was her compassion and sheer courage that saved her nephew, Marcos, who is mentally challenged, from the brutality of a psychiatric hospital. A series of unfortunate events left Marcos overworked and confused when he was accused of stealing from the Assembly of God church, where he performed light duties after the service. These events led him to have a total mental breakdown and he smashed the church's altar to pieces. He was sectioned and forgotten until Iracy fought with the psychiatrists and brought him to live with her. Slowly and patiently, she nursed him back to health. He is now able to live a regular life and is capable not only of taking care of himself but also his elderly mother.

Iracy's last act of kindness happened when Maria started to lose blood.

As I write I can still see my Auntie Maria sitting next to me at a big party my younger brother, Wilson, threw to celebrate our *Mamae's* 80th birthday.

Iracy was in her element, full of life with all her family around her. Even cousins from Serrania and the surrounding areas of Minas Gerais took the coach down to São Paulo for the occasion.

I noticed that Auntie Maria was restless, not herself, and making too many trips to the toilet.

'Auntie, are you unwell, please tell me, what can I do?'

'Kirinha, I am in a lot of pain and bleeding.'

'Oh my God, Auntie, let me take you to the hospital right away.'

'No! Look at her, look at your mother's happiness, you are here to celebrate with her, you came all the way from the United States.'

'England, Auntie Maria, in Europe'

'We wait until tomorrow morning. I cannot take his happiness from Iracy.'

Iracy had just turned eighty. She took Maria to endless appointments with various specialists, always demanding that her sister received the right diagnosis and treatment. After several stays in hospital, when the precarious medical services could no longer help Maria and she was sent home, it was Iracy who nursed her. The tasks involved were physically very demanding on Iracy's ageing, small frame as well as emotionally draining. She took on the responsibility with her usual fierce determination. Francoise helped as much as she could; she had to continue working full-time as a hairdresser. To watch her mother slipping away from her was, at times, emotionally draining. Iracy grasped what her niece was going through, and many times encouraged her to go out for a bit of distraction.

'Auntie, are you sure you don't need me to stay and help?'

'No, please go, have a break, have some fun Francoise, we will be fine, and we need our sisterly time together.'

'Auntie, please stay in my room, I will change the bed, put on some fresh sheets and leave you extra blankets.'

Francoise would return in the early hours to find Iracy on the floor next to Maria's bed. She could not leave her sister's side; she slept badly on the floor, always alert when her sister needed her throughout the night. She made her sister as comfortable as possible until it was impossible to care for her at home.

Without medical insurance there was no hospital or hospices that would take Maria in, to die with dignity and free from pain. The scene that unfolded will never leave my memory for as long as I live.

One morning, knowing too well that Maria did not have long to live and witnessing her deterioration and her suffering, Iracy called a taxi, picked up her sister and asked the taxi driver to drive them to the nearest hospital. They arrived at the hospital lobby, two old ladies, one carrying her dying sister and begging them to take her in.

'Please call the hospital manager, my sister is dying, she is in too much discomfort and pain. I can no longer take care of her at home. Please help us.'

Maria was taken in and given a bed and morphine to make her comfortable. Iracy sat by her side holding her hand, watching her sister carefully for any sign of discomfort.

'I am worried about you, Iracy, you look tired, and I doubt if they will give you a bed next to mine old girl, you still have a lot of living to do. Please go home now and rest. You have done all you can. I am comfortable now, the pain is under control, I am in safe hands. Go, Iracy, go.'

She kissed her sister goodbye and went home with her son Wilson, who was always there when his mum needed him the most. News of Maria's hospitalisation and imminent death travelled fast through Vila Maria and the Assembly of God's congregation; family members from all parts of São Paulo and even Minas as well as the churchgoers started to arrive at the hospital. Iracy left wondering; where all those people were when she was single-handedly nursing her dying sister? She was glad when she saw Maria's oldest son, Andre, walking into the hospital to pay his mum his respects. Andre had not visited his mum in years. No one knew that it was Iracy, with the help of her sons, who traced Andre and ensured he saw his mother one last time. Later, during one of my visits as we caught up on each other's life events, she shared: 'I did not do this for him. I did it for my sister. She had gone through enough and even in her darkest hour of pain and despair, she cried, scared of dying without saying her farewells to her eldest son.'

A few weeks after her death, Andre appeared at *Mamae's* house. It soon became clear that the sole purpose of his visit was to see if there was any money left for him.'

'Get out of my house, I don't want to see your face here ever again. She is gone, let her rest in peace, don't make me do anything to you that I might regret.'

She did not attend the funeral until the last minute when Maria was buried. She did not care for the shouting prayers and all the mourning, and at times hysterical crying which followed Maria's burial.

She was indeed, through her actions, practicing every religion under the sun and, without even knowing it, following the current Dalai Lama's teachings. She had the strongest and kindest heart of anyone I have ever met.

My younger brother once said that her genius was in her simplicity, her lack of ego and her ability to take the right action at the precise time without over analysing, without too many words or justification.

She aged fast after her sister's death, the shine always present in her eyes, that fire in her belly began to fade. She was already eighty-one years old.

The mother of honey becomes a mother in her own right.

After they were married and left the church, they went to live in a satellite town in Greater São Paulo, called Osasco. Odecio was making a good living and did not want Iracy to work. He was happy with the time and affection she showered upon him. He felt secure, loved at home and was enthusiastic about his work. Life was good. But soon Iracy was pregnant.

Cesar was born at home. A traditional midwife delivered him. Odecio had arranged everything to ensure Iracy, who was living far from her family, had the support she needed while he worked.

The distance a newborn creates between a man and his wife, and the sense of abandonment many new fathers feel, goes undetected to this day. It is still a taboo subject. Fathers experiencing these confusing emotions are unable to share them with anyone. The male conditioning of never showing any weakness prevents most men from speaking out or seeking help. Back in 1952, what a man felt and how he coped was not on anyone's radar, let alone Odecio's.

As for Iracy, motherhood meant exactly what her sister Ana Maria Luisa described when holding baby Gilberto. She also felt that it would not be possible to feel this unbelievable amount of love for anyone else, Aww, the purity and divinity of this love. If there was a heaven it must feel like this.

Odecio watched his young wife holding her baby and he knew he had been instantly replaced. The little orphan inside, with his almighty need for her love, started to stir.

Cesar soon grew up to be a very spirited boy. He played football like no other and was often being called to join teams all over our neighborhood. In his teenage years he would teach himself to play guitar, writing his own songs. My mum used to tell me that Cesar spoke when he was just seven months old. One morning she heard a voice calling her name and to her astonishment it was coming from baby Cesar's cot; he then proceeded to call Odecio's name, very loud and clear. But to me, his only sister, he gave me two special gifts; the first was how he tried to fiercely protect me from Odecio's outbursts – he did not fear him, their relationship was problematic to the very end, and the second was to open the windows of my young mind to new ways of thinking, challenging the status quo. He shared his passion for new artists, new music and literature, with all of his young siblings; it was the 1960s and a brand-new world was emerging. Cesar was in the middle of it all with his hungry and intelligent mind.

Soon her second son, Heathcliff, was born. Iracy was reading *Wuthering Heights* and decided to call her son after the central character. My brother Heathcliff has a deep mysterious nature to him. He devours books and to me is a professor in his own right. Heathcliff has a wicked sense of humour. We were the middle children, always fooling around, which we still do to this day. When he is in love, he writes beautiful poetry. Luckily, he is in love often.

I was born three years later and named Walkiria. I believe she liked the name but was not aware that the Valkyries were the angels of death who carried dead warriors to Valhalla. Where I now live, this is a very unusual name, and I am often asked about its origins. The angel of death is not very appealing to some.

Wilson, her last son, was born just eighteen months after me. Once again, she did not give her youngest son a typically common biblical name. But to us he was Nene and we adored him. He was a wholesome, beautiful baby boy. We all loved taking care of him. Although he was the baby, he was responsible and wise beyond his years. An early riser, he would walk to the bakery and fetch fresh bread and coffee for our breakfast. He has achieved a lot in his life. And just like Iracy and Odecio, Wilson and his wife Vania helped and housed many along the way. He plays the guitar beautifully and is also a writer. Later in his life he achieved his dream of an education, went to university and became a lawyer!

When I asked why she gave us all such different names, she said that she did not like the fact that all her sisters were called Maria something or had Maria as their middle name, combined with the fact that their surname was Silva – as common as Smith – so she decided to spice things up a little with her own children.

Although we all went to school there was no guidance or enforced discipline from Iracy to keep us on track. I often wonder whether her negative school experience had left her disillusioned with the whole idea that poor kids could get a dignified education. Iracy's reality was harsh, always a quest for survival, and perhaps our educational needs were left to teachers and the education system available to kids like us.

I often wonder why my father's relationship with his elder sons was so volatile. Wilson and I experienced a much greater love from our father. To us he seemed gentler and a lot more caring. He was also a much-loved grandfather.

We are under the illusion that parents bring their children up in the same way. But if we dig deeper, it cannot be so. The first born arrives to very inexperienced and younger parents, and the children that follow will arrive in an environment already changed by the first child. If we add to that mix many other influencing factors such as the ever-changing relationship of the parents, life events impacting the parents and children combined with the nature of each child, then it becomes clear that no child is parented in the same way.

Cesar, Heathcliff and Wilson will no doubt have their own different perspectives of growing up in our household being parented by Iracy and Odecio. Each one of them has a story that would stop your heart. My brothers and I grew up trying to do the best we could within our limitations, just like Iracy and Odecio.

The Mother Bear

Deep within Iracy lay a creature of feral ferociousness. The Mama Bear. No one messes with a Mama Bear who is protecting her family.

As a mother, she was not as sweet as her indigenous name suggests. She was not affectionate or over-protective. However, she was a mother bear in every sense of the word.

She was never a disciplinarian and allowed us a lot of freedom – perhaps a bit too much – and I have very few memories of her being angry or telling me off.

My very early memories of her are getting up at the crack of dawn to take my older brothers, Cesar and Heathcliff, to various clinics and hospitals to obtain specialist treatment for their eye conditions. She fought hard with an inadequate health system to get her sons the best possible treatment. We usually took several buses to reach distant hospitals and medical centers. We got there before daybreak and joined the queues already forming. To me, when we set off to a distant medical center or hospital, it was an adventure. I loved getting up in the middle of the night when everyone was still asleep. The streets were empty and lonely apart from just a few stray dogs, cats and homeless children, trying to sleep as best they could huddle in street corners and doorways, and the usual drunks who could not find their way back home the night before. The air was cooler and felt almost fresh before the sun came out and exhaust fumes added to the heat. As soon as we got a safe place in the queue, we would take turns to go to the nearest bakery for our breakfast. To me that was such a treat. We would order a *pingado* – today I guess this would be called a latte in most capitals of the world – and a sweet bread: a huge, sweet bun with sugar icing and custard cream inside. With our bellies filled with lattes and sweet breads, we would return to the queue. It took hours for the center to open and organise all the patients to be seen on the day. We played a lot around the grounds, running, skipping, hide and seek, always returning to the queue where Iracy patiently waited her turn, always ready to offer us some water, some oranges and some sad-looking bananas melting in the heat. In addition to the flip-flops, she had the habit of carrying a few oranges in her bag and a long, sharp knife to peel them with. As I write I remember how much trouble she caused when she visited the Tower of London. It was a hard task to explain to the security guards why she was carrying a knife, especially as no one in England uses a killer knife to peel oranges.

I have early memories of suffering with chronic stomach pains. I must have been about three or four as we still lived in Rua Lavapes. It was carnival time. As the pain got worse, Iracy and Odecio took me to the hospital. When we got there, it was a bit deserted. During the carnival celebrations, Brazil almost stands still for four days and four nights.

Odecio was carrying me as I whimpered in pain. The receptionists and some nurses were chatting and jigging to the latest carnival tunes playing on the radio. As we approached them, they took little notice of us.

'She needs to be seen straight away, she has been in pain since the early hours,' pleaded Odecio, his voice already raised. They continued to ignore him, making a dismissive gesture for him to sit down and wait.

He handed me to Iracy, walked back to the reception and started to throw all their books, trays and leaflets on the floor.

'You bunch of good for nothings, can't you see my baby girl is unwell and needs to be seen straight away?' His voice reached a dangerous level and he stared at them, shouting even louder, 'Get me a doctor now or I will drag one of you by the hair until you take us to him!'

We were seen straight away. I was medicated, and the pain stopped.

Odecio, the Daddy Bear!

Iracy was bursting with pride. She was glad to have her husband by her side. On the way back, they laughed and chatted as they relived the events at the hospital.

As I was feeling better, on the way home they stopped at a children's carnival ball.

I had been ill for so long they thought they could not pass a kid's carnival ball without taking me in, if only for a little while.

The hall was decorated with balloons, with paper streamers and many other decorative artefacts hanging from the ceiling. The music was loud, with popular carnival songs being played one after the other. The children's entertainers spotted my parents at the front door holding me and soon came over, whisking me away to the dance floor with the other children.

I remember feeling a little dizzy, awkward at first, but I was soon jumping to the music with the other children whilst my eyes fixated on where my parents were standing, watching me and chatting. Suddenly I ran from the dance floor towards them.

'What happened? Don't you want to play and dance the carnival with the kids?'

'I do but the elastic in my pants broke, and I want to go home.'

They laughed and laughed, picked me up and took me home. I felt happy, pain-free and invincible in my father's arms.

I often wondered if Iracy's diligent care with our health and regular check-ups was linked to her witnessing her young siblings and Ana Maria Luisa die due to lack of adequate medical care.

The mother bear would strike and protect me so many more times. Too many to mention here.

In the third year of Primary School, I had a teacher called Dona Fernanda. I disliked her immensely. I knew the feeling was mutual. She was always on edge. A small woman with light-brown hair. She had a red face and a habit of talking at the children with a painfully controlled irritability, passive anger escaping from every pore. When she lost her temper, she shouted at the entire class. In one of her angry outbursts, I mimicked her facial expressions when she wasn't looking, making the entire class burst out laughing. Every time she turned to face the class, I stopped and when she turned, I would carry on, and the kids would laugh. These little games of mine went on for a while until she turned suddenly and caught the offender.

She made me sit in front of the class. I obeyed. At the end of the school day as I was about to gather my things and walk home, she started shouting at me, grabbing both of my ears. She pulled them up hard, so hard I saw stars and started to cry in pain and fear of the mad woman I had to call my teacher.

'Don't you ever make a fool of me in front of the class again, do you hear me?' She continued to pull up my ears – passive anger now turning into full-blown anger. I managed to get out of her grasp and run out of the classroom in floods of tears.

I arrived home disheveled, my little ears burning and as red as Dona Fernanda's face.

Still crying, I told my mum what had happened.

She said nothing, gave me a glass of milk with sugar and sat with me quietly for a while.

I knew that when she went silent she was plotting something. She was secretive, never revealing her maleficent plans to anyone.

The following day, she woke up singing a joyful tune. She took me to school.

She never took any of us to school. She showed us how to get there on the first day and left us with the responsibility. So, I was delighted to be taken to school by my mother. We chatted happily all the way there. She shared with me a few things about her brief time at school and how much she loved her teacher. She had never met Dona Fernanda, I thought.

'Show me your teacher.'

I pointed to her in front of the class greeting the children. She walked right up to Dona Fernanda and without saying a single word slapped her hard across the face several times.

'Don't you ever touch my girl again. If she misbehaves, let me know.' I wanted to die of embarrassment! Then, turning to me: 'If you ever disrespect your teacher or misbehave in class again, you will get the same treatment.'

And just like that, with purposeful steps and her head held high, she walked out of the classroom. I sat there hearing her tiny steps walking away – flip-flop flip-flop.

Don't mess with my Mama Bear.

Keeping it real – a little too real

Birthdays were not celebrated in our home. There was no great fuss or high expectations of upcoming birthdays. Sometimes, Auntie Maria would come over and bake a cake, other times I was given some small change to buy sweet bread and a *pingado* on the way to school.

We were never allowed to believe in Father Christmas. I remember being told that to allow poor children to believe in Father Christmas was an unwise choice that could disappoint them. Odecio always preached that father Christmas was Uncle Sam's capitalist invention to make the poor greedy for useless goods they did not need. We knew that it was our parents who got us presents when they could. If they were having a difficult time and there were no presents, we knew our reality and there was never any disappointment. We did get into trouble, however, telling other children that Santa was a farce and did not exist.

At Christmas Odecio would bring home a hamper from his work filled with luxury goods that we only saw once a year: Brazil nuts, raisins, fancy chocolates, panettone and other goodies we all enjoyed. He would arrive late on

Christmas Eve looking filthy in his mechanic's overalls and exhausted, but happy to come home with the Christmas hamper for us. That Christmas hamper was one of his few perks.

Every Christmas Iracy would buy a large *pernil*: a leg of pork. She would marinate it during an entire night with spices, vinegar, lemon, garlic and onions, and then roast it slowly for Christmas lunch. Even though at times the festivities were clouded by drunken outbursts and pointless fights, I have some fond memories of all her attempts to make it a special occasion for us. She would queue for hours at certain charitable institutions that offered toys for the children of the less fortunate. She never hid this fact from us. I knew that Father Christmas did not exist, but I also knew that my parents were very real. I was aware of how hard she and my father tried to give us the best they could.

Iracy never put up a Christmas tree. I remember once she somehow brought home a beautiful white Christmas tree, and with her help we decorated it to perfection. It was a magical moment and a real novelty as we had never had one before. I used to look through other people's windows and admire their Christmas trees, the way they celebrated Christmas with presents and a very fake Father Christmas arriving after midnight. The kids' stupidity believing in this old, overweight saintly man dressed in red, arriving at their house once a year, never ceased to amaze me. I learnt from a very early age how easy it is to fool the innocent.

I will never know why, when Odecio arrived from work and saw Iracy and the four of us all gathered around our lovely, freshly decorated white Christmas tree, he became possessed with rage. He could see that the five of us were happy enjoying a new experience and some innocent Christmas cheer. Instead of joining in the fun, in a fit of anger he tore down the Christmas tree, pulling it apart and ripping it to shreds with all the decorations flying around the room. There was an uproar of screaming, shouting and crying from us.

'Leave our tree alone, why are you doing this?'

'To show your mother that she cannot treat me like a dog in my own house.'

'How is she treating you like a dog? How can the Christmas tree have anything to do with it?'

'When was the last time that she got me anything or showed me even a bit of affection?'

We had heard his lamentations before. I was saddened and exhausted by his outbursts. I could not contain my unhappiness and unashamedly burst into tears.

In her usual manner she calmed us down.

'It is done now. We can't bring the tree back. At least the five of us had a precious afternoon together, decorating and enjoying our little white tree. Your father's monstrous actions just show who he really is, now go outside and play.'

She cleared up and nothing more was said about it. He then, as he always did after these outbursts, sat at the kitchen table with his head on top of his folded arms as if hiding from us; hiding from the shame of what his uncontrollable temper was capable of. Hiding from the harm he had just caused us, and of course himself. At times like this, I would hover around him,

and he would lift his head just enough for me to see that he had been crying. I don't know what hurt me more, his angry outbursts that had the power of destruction or the devastating sadness that would follow, haunting him for days.

After such outbursts no one would have anything to do with him, so he would just sit there at the kitchen table, folded in half, hiding his shame. Such a pitiful sight. I am certain that he always hoped Iracy would take a small step towards him to try and console the emotional chaos always bubbling on the surface of his being. As usual, I could not bear to see him in such disrepair.

'*Papai*, it is getting late, wake up, it is getting dark outside, come sit in the lounge, watch some telly.' I would plead until he slowly got up, red-eyed, trying hard to compose himself. It broke my heart to see him like this.

As I write I reflect on how unfair life was for him. He never received any help to deal with that hungry ghost inside of him and the feeling of abandonment that accompanied him throughout his life. But I knew that there was a tender and compassionate part of his heart that touched mine many times.

On the cold nights during São Paulo's winter, Odecio could not settle until he checked on my young brother and me. We slept in the lounge, which, apart from a side door, was very open with no other doors to stop the draft: Wilson and I shared the sofa bed. During those cold winter nights, he would quietly open the kitchen door trying not to wake the house, and step outside, returning with a couple of bricks. He would place them in the oven to warm them up, wrap them in some old towels and place them on the sofa bed, underneath the thin covers, to keep us warm. He would get all the woolly jumpers and the few coats we possessed and put them on top of us. He would watch us for a while and stroke our hair.

'Ah, it is a lot warmer now, go back to sleep little ones, *meus tesouros*, sleep with angels.'

Our house in the middle of our street

Odecio was now working for a reputable national company. He oversaw their fleet of motor vehicles, including lorries. He was getting enough to support his family.

I have hazy memories of an old, almost derelict, house we rented in the centre of São Paulo. I remember *Mamae* in the kitchen busy with her chores and how she was always chasing the pigeons, who would enter the kitchen through holes in the roof and torment her. As I was still a pre-verbal child, being near these birds gave me the ability to copy their cooing sound to a T. I soon perfected their soft throaty sound, even making the same swelling of the throat. This is my party trick to this day.

But my vivid memories and the many stories still so alive in my mind happened when we moved to a rented house at Rua Assungui, which was a very long street joining two neighbourhoods. In addition to small family houses, it had three factories that polluted the air we breathed.

I can still picture the upheaval of the move, the chaos of boxes, bags of clothes and my parents' nervous energy. There was excitement in the air. We were finally leaving that old, dark house to a brand-new rented house filled with sunlight, freshly-painted walls, wooden floors, two big bedrooms, a lounge, kitchen, bathroom with a corridor running alongside it, a patio area at the back of the house with a tub for washing clothes and a small concrete area in the front of the house. It was next to a field, which housed a tower of power lines. Next door on the left was a house the same as ours, belonging to Dona Irene and her children. We would become lifelong friends of this family. Our landlord owned all of this and his own large, beautiful house on the same street where he lived with his daughter and two granddaughters. To us children, he was the richest man in the world. His immaculate granddaughters never came out to play with us in the street. They walked past our house from school every day and not even once managed a hello.

> *Four brand-new lives*
> *Four brand-new hearts*
> *Pumping and Mixing*
> *Tupi-Guarani, African and European blood*
> *Four pairs of eyes*
> *Four pair of ears*
> *Watching and listening*
> *Growing and learning*
> *at Rua Assungui*
> *a Tupi native Brazilian name meaning*
> *Blood running through veins*

Odecio and Iracy's union was a complex yet strong one. Throughout their fifty-four years of marriage, there were countless acts of immense love and dedication as well as countless acts of mutual cruelty.

There was an angry, abandoned, twisted inner child within Odecio. There was a hard-hearted, at times vindictive, inner child within Iracy. Yet despite their troubled and brutal childhoods, they were also survivors. They had to fight every day for their survival and now for the survival of their four children.

Ours was a busy, untidy house, always full of kids running around. Iracy loved children and they loved her. She was never a disciplinarian. Motherhood presented her with the opportunity to reinvent a childhood that was taken away from her far too soon. Kids would come to enjoy her famous *fuba* cake. Under her precise instructions, at the precise time, we would climb the fence to pick sweetcorn from the landlord's back garden. She climbed the fence herself early one morning, to the power-line fields next to our house, made a small vegetable patch, and planted yams and other root vegetables I can't recall. We enjoyed the yams for many years and so did my Auntie Maria who was by then living not far from us.

Our house was always bursting with life. So much went on in that house, in that street as the four of us grew up becoming teenagers and young adults.

There is no doubt in my mind about the love my parents both felt for their children. Winnicott, the English pediatrician and psychoanalyst, said that for a child to thrive all that is needed is a good enough mother or significant other in the child's life. In the greater scheme of things, considering the childhood traumas they both carried around, Iracy and Odecio were to me, much more than good enough parents.

The impact their volatile relationship had on their children is a different story.

I have fond memories of the times when they were playful and loving towards each other, always mimicking everyone and talking their secret code language they made up by using the syllabus and sounds of words backwards. Other memories I am still trying to make sense of to this day.

Over time, with great care and dedication, Iracy broke the concrete at the front of the house, dug up the soil and started what eventually became a beautiful garden. She planted a rubber tree, which grew to a healthy height with shiny leaves; it was a striking looking tree that produced a perfect red flower in spring. She also covered the garden with daisies. When the garden blossomed to its full glory it became a sight to behold in our street. Rua Assungui was a very long road, which housed three factories; there was virtually nothing of nature in that part of São Paulo, just more and more factories popping up and more and more cars invading the streets. Factory workers, neighbours and mothers with their schoolchildren would walk past our house and stop to admire her garden, her pride and joy. When the time was right, and the flowers were about to die, she would cut them and give them to the neighbours or the admirers passing by. She would cut them with so much joy.

'There you go, place them in a vase with tepid water – not too cold and not too hot – with a spoon of sugar and enjoy their beauty a little longer, I would hate to see my daises go to waste.'

People would come from all over to get some of her daisies. During these exchanges, she became alive: useful information was shared during this simple act of giving and receiving flowers.

I remember a spring when her garden blossomed to its full glory; a stunning red flower unfurled from the rubber tree. Odecio and Iracy had been fighting more than usual during that spring. Sometimes they would argue for weeks about things that had happened in the past, mixed with recent events, unknown to me, and everything else in between. It had been one of those dark and hurtful weeks between them. On Sunday, she took me to the street market. I recall it being quite a long walk and the whole expedition took most of the morning. Upon our return, we noticed to our horror that the garden had been destroyed – all the dazzling daisies dug up, the beautiful rubber tree butchered and thrown on the side, its magnificent red flower withering fast under the blazing sun. All that beauty

167

created by the labour of her love and her need for nature was gone in a flash on a sunny Sunday morning; instead, there were only rocks, ugly hateful rocks, covering the ground.

We both stopped outside our house, frozen and in shock. I looked at her with trembling lips, fighting the tears. I noticed that her eyes went very cold.

'You listen to me; we will walk into the house and pretend that nothing of great significance has happened this morning. We will not mention a word about what he has done to get at me. Do you understand? We shall not give him the reaction and the satisfaction he is waiting for.'

And in we went, she sang her little tunes and put the shopping way. She started to make the Sunday dinner as if nothing at all had happened, as if her beautiful garden, which she loved and took such great care of, her pride, her tiny piece of heaven, her little square of rural Minas Gerais – a bit of her roots she tried to create in the concrete jungle she now called home – was still there decorating the front of her house.

Odecio was inside expecting her reaction, but he got no acknowledgement or drama from her, just her cold dismissal of him that always cut through his soul.

To this day I don't know what the fight was all about or why he had retaliated in such a brutal way. Neither of them ever won those fights. They were both losers every single time.

For a long time, I walked past what used to be her garden with a heart full of ugly rocks.

Life went on as usual. Despite Odecio's job, his wages could not keep up with the constant rise of inflation. We lived under the constant fear of eviction. It was not always possible to pay the rent but somehow, at the very last minute, after the last eviction letter was posted through the door, Odecio managed to find some extra work and keep a roof over our heads.

Our house was pure organised chaos. Iracy was not house-proud, she did what she could. She preferred a house where her children could play, jump on the sofa, and have friends around. She allowed us strange pets, even though they were rather peculiar and had tragic ends, which broke our hearts.

She had fun with her children, always very involved in their activities. She seemed to know what was going on with us and our friends. I remember the hours she spent on rainy days reading the adventures of the Walt Disney characters to us. She made great voices and interpretations of Donald Duck, Mickey, Minnie, and Uncle Scrooge. Sitting by her side, listening to her reading and showing us the pictures in the comic books, I felt as if I was entering a new universe of stories with colourful characters and twisted plots full of danger and fun. She laughed with us at the funny endings and sometimes her voice sounded heavy, as if she had a lump in her throat, as I sobbed at the sad parts of the Disney fairy tales with the tragic fate of the princesses at the hands of wicked evil witches. She used to mutter under her breath cursing the stupidity and weakness of the gullible princesses for placing their trust and fates in the hands of the wicked. Puzzled, I would ask her: '*Mamae*, but what could they have done?'

'Well, they should not be such pathetic, weak imbeciles and find a way to poison them first!' She said these words with passion before going back to the story.

As we grew up, my brothers started to make friends of their own and play outside more and more. One day she noticed me playing with my Boogie Woogie talking doll all alone on the pavement.

'Why don't you ask Toquinho, Rosana or Regina next door to come and play with you?'

'They are not allowed to play with me.'

'But why not?' I could hear her voice rising.

'They say it is because I have three brothers and the house is always filled with boys.'

She said nothing, just sat there with me for a while, then she grabbed Boogie Woogie from me and cradled the dolly in her arms, looking at her affectionately: 'Well, well, Boogie Woogie, my little granddaughter, you have been playing a lot, you need a good bath and that dress needs a good wash as well.'

I followed her inside the house, laughing at the grandmother's voice she put on, high-pitched and breathy. At times like this, she became my friend. We bathed the dolly, wrapped her in a towel so she would not catch a cold, washed her tiny clothes and hung them on the line to dry.

A few weeks later she proudly announced that she had arranged for the little girls on the street to come to our house with their mums for a Doll's Birthday Party. She explained that she was going to make a *fuba* cake, popcorn, sweetcorn on the cob, fried sweet dough balls sprinkled with sugar and cinnamon and a jar of my favourite tangerine squash. The mums would bring their daughters with their dollies and a plate of party food.

My heart was racing, something magical exploded inside of me. I ran to her and hugged her. She had been to see each mum on the street who had a daughter about my age and explained her plight of having an only daughter and three boisterous boys.

The little girls arrived with their dollies; their mothers followed behind with a plate of party food. I noticed how shy and gentle the little girls were. I noticed how well-dressed the mothers were compared to mine. They had tried for the occasion. I rushed inside, washed my face with soap, brushed my hair and put a dress on in less than a minute. I did not want to look or behave like a boy. I had to make a good impression. Iracy noticed, smiled at me

171

and called me back into the kitchen and wiped my dirty knees with a damp cloth.

'There, you are as pretty as a picture, my beautiful girl.'

She did not bother to run inside to smarten herself up. She could not care any less. The external never interested her. She had made low tables out of cardboard boxes, which she covered with real, colourful tablecloths she had made from the bits of material my Auntie Maria rescued from the factory's litter. The plates of party food were placed on the table already half full of Iracy's creations. She added leftover pineapple slices and watermelon chunks. Voila, we had ourselves a feast!

The mothers chatted. We girls ate and pretended to feed our dollies, sharing their names. Not long after, we were running about playing.

The party was a success. Although the girls were still not allowed to come over to our house very often, I received invitations to go to their houses.

To this day, I have no idea where she hid the boys for an entire afternoon.

My brothers, in turn, built carts made with planks of wood – *carrinho de rolimao* – and wheels; they played freely in the streets. They made their own kites with colourful papers, thin sticks and glue made at home with flour and water. They used to fly their kites for hours and hours. During bonfire season in June, which is the colder month in Brazil, they made balloons out of several patches of thin translucent paper in various bright colours, glued together, with inside frames of thin wire and a wire loop around the bottom opening holding a paraffin soaked pad; for us kids and even some grown-ups, it was thrilling to watch the little lit balloons go up and up giving the night a touch of magic, creating a warm festive feel at Rua Assungui. I would join all the other kids running after the colourful lanterns, making the night sky come alive.

Across the street there was an empty plot of land and all the boys, my brothers included, decided to build a tent and make it their headquarters for important strategic meetings. They loved the hideout, which was useful on boring rainy days. One morning they woke up to find it destroyed, with all their wooden carts, marbles and ropes gone. I can't begin to describe the pandemonium that followed. All the boys were screaming, shouting and plotting to find and beat up the culprits. Iracy, of course, was very involved and outraged. I must have been seven years old at the time; very skinny, shy and small for my age. I watched the spectacle on the sidelines, sad for my brothers. They loved the hideout they built from scratch. It turned out that a much older boy with bullish tendencies had caused the destruction. He was part of a bigger gang of boys, so to take him on would have been disastrous to the younger boys. Iracy watched the developments with quiet and determined curiosity. A few days went by, and the boys learnt to live with their disappointment. One day, when the older boy appeared in the street, showing off with his usual arrogant manner in front of all the kids out playing, she turned to me with this massive piece of wood with a few nails stuck in it that she had prepared herself with no one knowing. She handed it to me. When she saw the horrified look on my face, she gave me a serious look and proceeded with very precise instructions.

'Now, what you are going to do is wait until he turns around, then I want you to approach him but hide the stick behind your back and then hit him several times in front of everyone.'

'But I don't want to hurt him, *Mamae*.'

'Go, he needs to be taught a lesson.'

'Why can't the boys do it?' My voice quivered. My eyes welled up.

So, I mastered all my courage, walked up to him when he was not looking and smashed the stick with the nails across his back several times. He was so shocked and so was I; we looked at each other in terror!

Then all the boys cheered and laughed, whistling and calling him names.

'You got ambushed and beaten by a little girl, what are you going to do now?'

As they laughed and mocked him, I ran back to Iracy, running inside of the house and crying my eyes out. I felt terrible committing such a violent act and being part of a drama that had nothing to do with me. I intended to hide indoors forever to avoid that boy and not be part of Iracy's little schemes ever again.

But her malevolent plan worked. Another hut was built, and their wooden carts, marbles and ropes returned. Peace was restored in Rua Assungui once again.

I have many fond memories of growing up the only girl in a household dominated by three active boys. But my most vivid and treasured memories are of the unusual, even bizarre, pets we shared.

The first one was a little epileptic cocker spaniel whom we named Pitoco, due to his lack of a tail. My dad brought him home. He was abandoned at the garage where he worked at the time. Wilson and I climbed to the kitchen table as we watched the little puppy whimper and shiver on the floor. To this day I have no idea what had happened in young Pitoco's life before he came to us. He was a nervous little dog, had these epileptic fits and could not walk in a straight line so he was always bumping into things. He could not have found a better home to take care of him. And take care of him we all did. We made up a little song, a kind of rap that sounded like a football chant, to call him home.

'Pitoco, come on home, Pitoco

Toco, come on home, Pitoco

Come on home, Toco Pitoco, Toco Pitoco.'

And he would appear from nowhere, trying to waggle the tail he didn't have, running towards us in his crooked little way, always crashing against the wall and peeing everywhere from the excitement of seeing us chanting away his name.

He was a great little performer too. At the dinner table he would dance, howl and show his teeth to get a bit of our dinner.

On the days the dog catchers appeared on our street looking for stray dogs, we would all rush in a panic looking for him and pleading to the horrible men with their nasty dog nets to leave our Pitoco alone.

But all good things must come to an end. One day he did not return despite our tuneful and rhythmic calls. He went missing for days. We stood outside taking turns, calling him, sometimes at the top of our voices.

'Pitoco, come on home, Pitoco

Toco, come on home, Pitoco

Come on home, Toco Pitoco, Toco Pitoco.'

We called and called him and hoped that he would appear running towards us wagging his stubby tail, crashing against the wall, pissing himself with excitement. But he never did.

I remember feeling anxious with worry for Pitoco. Time went by then one day Mum sat us down.

'I don't know how to say this, but Pitoco had one of his epileptic fits and this kind man took him to a nearby vet, where he died peacefully.'

It was such an obvious lie. Who would spend time and money on a sick dog in that part of the world. Sometimes, when the truth was too harsh, she tended to fabricate stories to make us feel better. I felt she realised we needed closure. I believe in two possible truths:

1. Pitoco was finally caught by the dog catcher and there was no money to pay the releasing fee and he died of starvation in the council's kennels. His little body was then boiled and turned into soap.

2. He was run over when trying to cross the road in his twisted little way and may have walked straight into the wheels of a moving car. Eventually his little smashed body was thrown in the garbage when he began to stink under the blazing sun.

There can be no other explanation. He was a much-loved little dog, but no one would bother to save him for he was a bit of a mess and riddled with fleas. We did try to wash him and keep him clean but there was no point. After being thoroughly washed with washing powder, he used to run and roll on the dirt and come back in a worse state.

In time our beloved little dog's horrible end stopped playing in my mind. But I can still sing and rap his calling song. So can my brothers.

Both Iracy and Odecio did not want any more pets. They could not bear to see us so upset when they finally went.

Our second and final pet had a much more tragic end. He was called Jose or Ze. We loved him just as much. He behaved pretty much like Pitoco. He would also come running when we called him. We would even secretly hide him in our beds, just like we did Pitoco, when it was too cold outside.

The problem was that Jose was not a dog but a cockerel.

One day at the fair we saw a big bag full of chicks. It was love at first sight, we wanted one.

"Mamae buys us a chick…look mamae, that poor little one is so cute and needs a home, Mamae, will you buy it? please?" Wilson and I begged.

"I told you four, no more pets. And a chick is not a dog and is not suitable for a pet. Let's go and don't cry."

Little did we know that Heathcliff, in a silent but sudden movement, feeling sorry for Wilson and me, had put the little yellow animal in his pocket without anyone noticing.

We were proud of our bizarre pets. No one in our street had had an epileptic little dog and now a domesticated cockerel that behaved just like an epileptic little dog.

However, Jose did not have a dignified end. He was murdered!

One evening *Mamae* called us in for dinner. The house smelt of delicious food. We all sat at the table and asked what was for dinner. She went silent. And we knew that the deliciously smelling dinner was Jose, our little Ze.

Wilson and I screamed at her.

'Murderer, Murderer, Assassin!!' We cried and refused to eat little Jose. I had seen her kill a chicken before and make a casserole in six easy steps. I knew Jose had been murdered in the same way.

1. She gently stroked him then she placed her right hand around his little neck and with one mighty twist broke poor Jose's neck.

2. She placed him in a pot of boiling water for hours.

3. She plucked his feathers, humming a little tune and singing one of her stupid little songs or the latest tune she had heard on the radio that morning.

4. She cut him open with a sharp knife – cleaned his guts.

5. She cut the rest of his little body into sizeable chunks.

6. She seasoned him, placed him in a pan with vegetables and turned him into a casserole.

Assassin – Cold Blooded Murderer

Wilson and I refused to eat Jose. The others simply ate our beloved pet cockerel and had our portions for seconds.

I cried myself to sleep with a hungry belly.

After that neither Wilson nor I wanted any more pets. We could not keep them safe in such an insane household!

A woman ahead of her times

With the needs of four children to navigate, life got hectic.

Odecio started to drink more than usual. Perhaps he needed some relief from his brutal routine and the heavy responsibilities placed upon his shoulders to pay the rent, pay the bills and put food on the table. That familiar hungry ghost inside of him was back with a vengeance. He felt neglected. He missed Iracy's attention.

Iracy reacted in the only way she could. Throughout her life she had witnessed the brutality of the men around her. Odecio's behaviour pressed all the wrong buttons in her hard-heartened inner child. She was never submissive; always ready to retaliate if necessary. The more she pushed him away, the more he longed for her affection and approval.

So, they danced their strange little dance of laughter and despair, of love and hate, of passion and indifference, while four brand-new lives, four brand-new souls watched on the sidelines.

The liberation from the Assembly of God's repressive doctrine freed Iracy and Odecio in so many ways. They loved music and movies. Odecio had an inquisitive mind. He spent his Sundays reading the papers, always sharing with us the latest national and world news. When we became puzzled or saddened about what went on in the world, he quoted Shakespeare: 'There are more things in heaven and earth, Horatio, than are dreamt of in your philosophy.'

Iracy could now wear her hair shorter and more stylish. She developed a passion for fashion and bright red lipstick. As a little girl, I used to love watching her dress up for parties and the many weddings and family gatherings. As if by magic she would transform from my tiny mum, always in her shabby housedresses, stained, damp apron and worn-out flip-flops, into a glamorous movie star. She wore tailored dresses and her hair up in a voluminous beehive type of hair do, but what I loved the most was her bright red lipstick. There was something daring and sensual about her on those occasions.

The only one who struggled with this transformation was Odecio. He would look at her and immediately sulk. He became more and more possessive of her.

Though he tried to repress and cage her
With all his mighty and eager needs
He was the one left in prison
By the power of her reason

She followed no one's orders, least of all her husband's.

I was always amazed at how she would bounce back from life's blows. For years she would hide her smile with her hands, embarrassed of her teeth rotting away in her mouth, giving her not only a destitute look but bad breath. She eventually found a government-subsidised dentist. She had been saving for ages. The day finally came. We went with her to this dentist. It was miles away: I remember a long walk from our house to catch a bus that dropped us just outside the dentist. We sat in the waiting area with some comic books she bought us. After what felt to me like an entire afternoon, she emerged. She had every single one of her rotten teeth removed in one go. Her mouth was stuffed with cotton, her face had ballooned with the swelling and her eyes were tearful. We followed her and crossed the road to wait for our bus. She held our hands, and I could feel she was trembling. We hopped on the bus; everyone was looking at us. She tried hard to wipe away the blood-stained dribble that the cotton wool could not contain. I felt embarrassed and full of sadness for her. But soon she was the proud owner of dentures and the freedom to smile with clean, fresh, minty breath.

Odecio had a different approach to dentistry. Although he was also having problems with his teeth due to lack of dental care, he was not as brave as Iracy and refused to go to the dentist. I have vivid memories of how he would take an unhealthy number of painkillers then ask for my assistance to help him remove the tooth that was troubling him. His method was simple but, to me, barbaric and I hated being his dental nurse. He would tie a thin piece of nylon string to his tooth – long enough to tie it to a door handle – then, when the nylon string was firmly tied to his tooth and the door, he would stand away from the door until the string was fully stretched and ask me to bang the door with all my might. I did as I was told, letting out loud screams of panic. I cannot remember if he ever succeeded in pulling a rotten tooth out, but I remember the blood everywhere in his mouth and him taking even more painkillers.

Iracy was growing in confidence. She enrolled herself on a course to learn to sew. At first my father had no problem with it for he thought it was just an excuse for women to gather and do some embroidery. When he realised that the course was teaching her to design dresses and giving her a skill, he felt uncomfortable with the whole thing. She loved the course and was a natural. Soon, she could make a dress, a shirt or anything she chose from scratch by measuring the person, drawing the design on paper, cutting the cloth and voila, her own beautiful creation was born.

Maria would bring her bits of textile they threw away at the factory where she worked. Iracy would create works of art with them.

To focus on her course and to keep us off the streets, as well as giving us some structure and a place to play and learn, she enrolled us in a children's play group run by the local council. She was heavily criticised for this; it was hard for her sisters, friends and acquaintances to comprehend how a housewife, whose husband could provide for her children, could possibly choose to follow a passion or learn a new skill. To them, her responsibility was to serve her family.

But as she never gave a damn about what people said or thought about her, we attended this playgroup for a few years before going to school. We loved it there: there were many activities, a swimming pool, arts and crafts and some boisterous crazy children just like us.

She was enjoying her course, and she was a natural. When she heard that the playgroup was putting on a show to honour the Tupi-Guarani culture and the indigenous people that had inhabited the southern estates of Brazil, she got involved with all her might and created some beautiful designs for the show – I have a feeling she was also honouring her mother and grandmother. She created dozens of outfits made of green satin and yellow paper to represent sweetcorn, which was cultivated by the Tupi tribes to make maize flour, their staple diet. This practice influenced Brazilian cuisine to the present day, including Iracy's famous *fuba* cake. After weeks of hard work bent over her sewing machine, she was ready to deliver all the outfits for the show.

The show was a spectacle of colour and movement, her perfectly designed outfits gleamed and shined as the kids moved and danced through their choreographed routines to the bumping sound of indigenous drums and melodic pipes.

She was in her element, chatting with all the teachers and mothers and proud of her children's participation in the grand event. She smiled shyly at the compliments pouring on her from the teachers, the mothers and the children.

'You made all this possible with your incredible designs, I never knew you had this gift.'

'Thank you, Iracy, for all the hard work you put into creating the outfits, they are just what was needed to bring the dance to life.'

I loved wearing her creations and danced my heart out for all to see. I thought my heart would burst.

Soon after the show, and without telling anyone, she applied for a job she saw advertised at a family wedding dress business. She carried out various tests with deep concentration and precision. She was invited to join the firm, not as a seamstress but as a supervisor to oversee the work of ten seamstresses. She came home elated.

'Odecio, I am over the moon, they really like my work and offered me the supervisor's role. The money is good. It will mean so much to our family. We could save and even buy our own home one day.'

'No wife of mine will go out to work. My kids will not be brought up on the streets.'

'But I can pay for someone to help. I will make sure everything is organised and the kids are taken care of.'

'It is a choice you will have to make. You take the job, I am out of the door, you will never see me again.'

She did not argue. She heard the stillness and determination in his voice. She saw the hurt in his eyes. She knew that fighting him on this occasion would mean dragging four innocent children through a war no one could win. I felt the defeat of her choice. I witnessed her internal struggle. I saw the twisted smile she presented the next day. I heard the pain in the happy songs she sang, trying to hide her disappointment. As hard as she tried, on this devastating occasion, she fooled no one.

As I write, I reflect on the fact that only a few decades later I would struggle with the opposite choice of leaving my own children behind, who were still babies, to go back to work. Women would gain more rights and autonomy, but the choices would remain just as hard.

You would think that she would never design clothes again after that blow to her dreams and ambition, but no, not her. Using me as her very patient model, she continued to make beautiful dresses inspired by the fashion magazines she loved so much. I feel that the world of fashion was her escapism from harsh daily life; I have fond memories of our time together when I would stand still and let her drape me in beautiful pieces of material – courtesy of Auntie Maria. After hours of cutting and adjusting her creations with pins I was free to go, but instead I sat by her sewing machine and watched her work with such concentration humming her little tunes. During those times, she shared a lot of stories from her past and tried to answer my endless questions about her life in Serrania.

For my first day at school, before we had to wear uniform, Maria collected various pieces of different shades of green material, bits of silk, patterned cotton and linen. Iracy spent ages putting the bits of material together until she formed a pattern she was happy with. She was left with a piece of material varying in texture and shades of green and created one of the most beautiful dresses a girl aged seven could possibly wish for her first day at Primary School. My heart was bursting with pride for my little mum, a creative genius of a fashion designer! My heart was also broken to leave her at the school gates; however, I got so many compliments for my dress that it made it a little easier to bear our first separation.

I told everyone she had made the dress, detailing the whole process of how she put the pieces of rags together to create the material, then drew the design on paper – a very complicated process that required precise drawing and the calculation of the measurements. I explained how she carefully cut the cloth to make the dress. One of the lunchtime helpers at the school asked me if my mum was a fashion designer and I immediately replied with a loud, 'YES, SHE IS!'

When she came to pick me up, I heard them point at her and laugh.

'Is this the fashion designer? She could at least create something decent for herself to wear.'

The sounds of their laughter cut through to the core of my seven-year-old being. I was beginning to understand more and more how cruel small and unkind minds could be.

I knew she had heard them, but she carried on asking me dozens of questions about my day and encouraging me to enjoy my time at school and choose carefully who I allowed to be my friend.

On another occasion, when I was about thirteen, she fell in love with a red dress she saw in a magazine. The magazine was called *Vogue* and was very expensive. She kept going back and looking at it. It was a brand-new fashion from Europe where dresses were mid-length with long puffed-up sleeves. It did look amazing in the magazine.

Time went on and I heard no more about the dress. Little did I know that Maria was under strict orders to find a piece of red material. When she finally found it, Iracy started to plan her design for the dress she had fallen in love with. None of us had any idea what *Vogue* represented in the world of fashion. Weeks later and after many hours of standing still while she drew the design from memory, cut the cloth and adjusted it on me, the dress was done. And it was splendid.

I can still see the red dress so vividly in my mind. It was a vibrant shade of velvety red, like the red of blood itself. It was of mid length with a gentle flair in the skirt that moved as I walked. It had long, tight sleeves that gave my arms an elongated look, slightly puffed up at the shoulders giving it a majestic air.

That beautiful dress was her best work of art, and I was honoured to be her model. I took great delight in parading like a model up and down our tiny house for her to admire her creation.

'And here is the red dream dress by the talented Brazilian designer Iracy, pay attention to the incredible detail of the regal sleeves and the movement of the skirt.' I joked around as I walked up and down my imaginary catwalk. She would laugh and blush a little.

Albert Einstein was so right when he quoted that intelligence will get you from A to B but imagination will get you everywhere; that afternoon our imaginations took us both to the catwalks of Europe.

I also had to wear the dress during one of our many trips to the rural parts of Minas Gerais where we spent some time with her cousins who had stayed behind. I felt very self-conscious wearing that sumptuous dress in such impoverished surroundings. But I did it for her and guess what? They loved it and were very proud of her and I am certain that a bit of colour and glamour brightened up their lives, if only for a little while.

She continued to copy beautiful designs and create them for me, sewing shirts for the boys and even her own glad rags for special occasions. I was always surprised and delighted by her transformation.

Years later, when I visited with my husband, she insisted on making him a shirt from scratch. And just like I used to model for her, he patiently stood there, that six feet of a man, letting her take his measurements, draw the design, cut the cloth and hold it against his torso, full of pins. It was a great shirt, and he wore it for years to come.

She made and adjusted garments for her family until her eighties when her eyesight started to fail her.

Odecio and Iracy continued to dance their unique dance inventing new steps as they went along.

He wore his passionate heart on his sleeve, giving us a window into his emotions. He felt for the poor and oppressed he saw all around us. He was always helping people, fixing their cars for nothing, taking the ill to hospitals, buying them groceries. He was also gregarious and full of mischief and still very much loved by Iracy's family, whom they visited very often.

Iracy had the same empathy and compassion, but she focused more on her family and cousins who had stayed behind in Minas Gerais and other rural areas of the country. There were many of them.

Now, looking back, Odecio and Iracy did not need to go to church to put into practice benevolence and compassion towards their less fortunate fellow humans.

The house, at countless times, also housed the lost, the desperate and the lonely.

I will never forget how Iracy housed, guided and protected Aparecida.

Aparecida was the sister of one of her cousins' husbands. No one really knows what prompted Aparecida to embrace the oldest profession in the world to earn a living.

Aparecida was only nineteen when she found herself pregnant. With nowhere to go, she knocked on her brother's door asking for shelter until she could work again. He refused to give her shelter but instead gave her a string of abuse and a black eye. When Iracy heard this story, she managed to find Aparecida: The sight of that poor young woman, a few months gone and showing, parading the red district in a tight dress, was a bit too much even for my mum to deal with. Aparecida was still working and trying to conceal her pregnancy. With no questions asked, she invited Aparecida to live with us until the baby was born and she could master a plan for her and the baby.

I remember Aparecida arriving at Rua Assungui with a tiny suitcase, in a bright-yellow dress already too tight around her bulging belly.

'When can we fetch the rest of your stuff?' Iracy asked her with a determined look on her face.

'All I have in the world is inside this case,' she touched her belly with a pensive look. 'And inside of me.'

I noticed straight away that she was white, without a hint of brown. She had a round face, big smile and very dark eyes and hair, making a striking contrast to her pale skin. The four of us were very excited to see her: a new person, a new tragic story to feed our imaginations. We took her case, held her hands, and led her to the sofa. Iracy brought her *fuba* cake, popcorn, sweetcorn on the cob and fried sweet dough balls dusted with sugary cinnamon and a fresh pot of coffee. We had a little party for her. She talked to us about the baby. She put our little hands on her belly and asked us to be quiet and wait. Then I felt a little kick; I was marveled by Aparecida and the life growing inside of her.

Our party was interrupted by Odecio's footsteps. When he saw us all fussing and laughing with Aparecida, he called my mum into the kitchen. He looked angry. He did not even glance at the young woman.

'Iracy, what are you doing? We can't have this whore in our house. What kind of example you are setting for our daughter? I want her gone.'

'She is here for the duration of her pregnancy, Odecio. She has nowhere to go, she can't work. Where is that heart of yours?'

'You choose now woman, if she stays, I will go.'

'Then collect your things and leave through the back door, Odecio, that young woman needs me.'

After the usual shouting match, the matter was settled and Aparecida stayed with us. Iracy found a Catholic institution run by nuns. She convinced them that she and Aparecida had been devout Catholics their entire lives. The well-rehearsed story she told the nuns to explain Aparecida's pregnancy will always be their secret. She had a little girl called Renata. Aparecida and her baby stayed with the nuns, learnt some vital life skills, found employment and eventually, lodgings for her and her daughter.

Not long after, Esmeraldo, Odecio's eldest brother, descended upon us with his lover. His wife, tired of his philandering, had finally thrown him out. One of the bedrooms where my older brothers slept was offered to them until they could find a place of their own. The four of us camped in the lounge.

There was no recrimination from Iracy's part. She accepted them both into her home. She was a compassionate, liberal-thinking host.

Esmeraldo was tall, much taller than Odecio. He was dark and handsome in a kind of haggard way. He was a talented guitar player, a carpenter by trade and an artist. He made amazing sculptures out of wood. We used to love listening to him playing his guitar and singing sad folk songs.

Things started going sour between the two brothers. They both liked a drink. When under the influence of alcohol, they became competitive; they even, for some bizarre reason, started a chili eating competition washed down by *pinga* – Brazilian firewater made from sugar cane – neither won the competition as they both ended up in hospital having their damaged stomachs pumped out.

One fine Christmas, we were sitting at the table enjoying Iracy's leg of pork, marinated overnight with lemon, vinegar, garlic, onions and spices, when Esmeraldo asked Iracy for another glass of wine. As she handed him the filled glass, Odecio launched at his brother, punching him to the floor and taking the tablecloth with him — as well as all the dishes, plates, glasses and cutlery, which all crashed to the ground.

Many accusations, supplications and lamentations were uttered by the adults, contaminating the air in our kitchen at Rua Assungui. After much persuasion by all of us, Odecio left his brother alone, who immediately took refuge in his room. Odecio sat at the table now deserted by everyone — holding his head in his hand crying. Iracy picked up the mess of broken plates and glasses. I helped her in silence, listening to my uncle Esmeraldo, now locked in his room, packing his cases.

When some order was restored to the kitchen, I left the house. I noticed my hands were trembling, my throat had this choking feeling and I had difficulty breathing, but I could not cry. I walked alone, peering inside other houses with Christmas trees, where children could believe in Father Christmas and fairy tales.

As I left home at a young age, I was able to take a helicopter view on my parents' behaviour. From afar, I was able to bring them down from that pedestal we tend to put our parents on as children. They became just two human beings, diving and ducking, in their human duality and I was able to love them in all their imperfections with no judgement but understanding, for what is love without understanding? This new-found perception brought forth an immense gratitude for the many acts of loving kindness they both bestowed upon me. Overall, I did well in the ovary lottery.

Another unforgettable Christmas stored in my heart happened when Odecio went to fix a car somewhere far away one Christmas evening, arriving a few minutes before five o' clock in his filthy overalls, his hands black with grease. He grabbed me by the hand as we ran together to the toy shop, arriving breathless. He stopped the shutters — which were already coming down — and begged the owner to let us in. He handed the shop owner an awful lot of money, his entire day's earnings, so that I could have the talking doll I had been drooling over on my way to school. Not even Father Christmas could have performed such a miracle. I felt as if my heart would explode with pride and love for this passionate, intelligent and giving father of mine. Our happiness was complete as we walked back home carrying a massive blue and pink box containing my first doll, who smelt of vanilla, dressed in a pink dress with a white pinafore, proper white shoes and pink socks; she had the cutest pink-white face with blonde curls and round, blue eyes – her name was Boogie Woogie the talking doll – made in the USA.

Boogie Woogie was an instant hit with my cousins. When I visited my grandmother with my brand-new imported doll, a long queue of children appeared to see and hear her. They pulled a little cord behind her back, and she would say in the sweetest melodic of baby voices:

'Mama
I want my bottle
Mama
I want water.
Mama
I want a nap'

Boogie Woogie was much-loved and lived a happy life until she lost her voice completely. Iracy found a place where they fixed talking American dolls. It took ages to get there. Iracy consoled me all the way there, reassuring me that her little granddaughter could be fixed. The doll repairer was kind and told me she was going to be very well looked after by him. Long weeks went by and then she was ready for collection.

We tested her there and she sounded fine, just a bit hoarse and her voice was deeper. Iracy told me she was growing up and her voice was changing, which made perfect sense to me at the time.

When we got home my brothers and other children were waiting to hear Boogie Woogie again. When I pulled the little cord at the back of her neck, she made a strange barking noise that had everyone in fits of laughter: it was wolf-like and in a very deep slow tone.

'I want my bottle!' she yelled, followed by more barking sounds.

The fits of laughter continued and despite my shock, I joined in. Boogie Woogie amused us until she could be fixed no more.

I loved Boogie Woogie; we would spend many afternoons sitting with her, watching cartoons and the shenanigans of my favourite children's programme that took place on a farm. The main characters lived in São Paulo but spent their holidays with their grandmother on a farm. I could relate to that. We also spent our holidays in rural Brazil with our relatives. Not on a farm, but in their tiny brick houses with no electricity or running water, sleeping on the floor, playing in the fields, gazing at the breath-taking unpolluted night skies covered by billions of stars and spotting the shooting stars. Just like Iracy did when she lived there.

She was always so happy back in Minas Gerais with her countless cousins, aunties and relatives who remained farm labourers in rural Brazil. It was delightful for me to sit among them listening to the stories of an era gone by.

We all left the idyllic fields of Minas Gerais, and our lovely relatives, with an inexplicable sense of loss and longing; they lived such impoverished existences, but their generosity of heart was a gift that money could not buy.

It wasn't until the middle of the 1960s that I started to see some fundamental changes happening in and out of our household. Cesar and Heathcliff were now teenagers. Their minds and hearts were open to the world around them. There was a strong feeling of rebellion in the air. Young people all over the world were rejecting old values and creating a new world for themselves.

The hippy movement was strong in São Paulo. Cesar and Heathcliff embraced it wholeheartedly, growing their hair, adopting the fashion at the time, and bringing new sounds from England and America. Although we did not understand the words, the music felt so free. It intrigued and liberated us at the same time. The Brazilian Tropicália movement brought us our own idols singing of love and peace and a new way of being.

But this cultural liberation did not reach its full splendor as Brazil was also experiencing times of repression due to the military dictatorship. We began to hear the first stories of cases of torture and disappearances. Our confused young hearts carried feelings of hope for a world of love and peace that our idols proclaimed, but also immense fear for the brutality that the military junta inflicted on anyone who dared disobey its monstrous and oppressive orders. There are too many cases of unimaginable cruelty that the junta committed against our students, artists, poets and writers to be mentioned here.

Inside our home at Rua Assungui tensions were also bubbling up between the old and the new. While Iracy embraced the changes and had no issues with the music, the fashion and the friends hanging around the house, Odecio could not understand the hippy and Tropicália movements. He hated the new music, the long-haired youth, the way they dressed and their dismissive attitude towards anything old. He did not know what to make of the likes of Jimi Hendrix, Bob Dylan or Caetano Veloso. This made Odecio fearful and confused. He was also aware of the drugs and their effect on the young. He became angry and intolerant of Cesar and Heathcliff.

Fights between my father and his first born began to turn ugly. Their constant shouting matches exhausted us all.

'If you want to remain under my roof, you will do as I say, you good for nothing', shouted Odecio.

'I am no longer that little boy you repressed and tried to make into you. I will never be like you, I detest even the air that you breathe, you, odious little old man.' We could feel the hatred pouring out of Cesar towards my father as he spat his venom.' I often wondered at times like this, how much of the anger they projected on each other was hugely influenced by alcohol and drugs. But I will be left forever wondering what my family would have been like if professional help was available; could the demons my father carried be comforted, or even healed? Would the trauma stored in Odecio's DNA haunt us forever?

The conflict between them got so bad that Cesar left home to join a hippy commune. He was not even allowed to come and visit us. I will never forget the feeling of emptiness and confusion that followed me like a black cloud after my brother left us. He left full of anger at the injustices he felt at home. He was also exasperated by the repressive events happening in Brazil at that time; everyone lived in fear under the military junta backed up by some evil and brutal military police. I felt so much tenderness for my brother Cesar; he was always standing up for us against Odecio's temper.

The morning after his departure from Rua Assungui, the whole house and neighbourhood felt numb. The space he occupied with his flamboyant and eager presence was too huge to go unnoticed and it just hung there in the middle of everything.

But after some time, he would come by and visit us, He would fill our world with stories of the hippy movement happening across the world and our own Tropicália movement, he would share new music, new books and endless stories of his new life. He had become a radical left wing anti-conformist.

Come to think of it, Cesar was not that different from the angry young man Odecio once was. He was life-curious, taking his uplifting energy with him wherever he went. However, Odecio in his later-life wisdom, wanted his sons to learn a trade, preferably following his footsteps into mechanical engineering. He knew how vital it was to be able to earn a living.

Cesar's anger, his alternative life style and militant attitude towards the military junta brought him a lot of trouble at the time. I hope he will write his own story one day.

The void in the middle of my being

I was just a bystander in the many unfortunate events that unfolded between my elder brothers and my father.

My family dynamics changed with Cesar's departure. I felt that Iracy could never forgive Odecio for the way he had treated Cesar. Odecio felt that Iracy always took the children's side and failed to support him in his many attempts to discipline us. I felt the distance between them grow faster each day and there were less and less moments of gaiety in their interaction. Now Heathcliff had become the scapegoat for Odecio's neurotic confusion. They fought continuously over stupid little things. Carl Jung highlighted that where the will to power and control is paramount, love will be lacking. However, Heathcliff stayed with my parents throughout his life; he had a different temperament; a sensitive yet gregarious nature, a sharp intelligence with a passion for philosophy and literature topped by a wicked sense of humour.

I have asked myself so many times why Odecio had such problems relating to Cesar and Heathcliff. I was too young to remember how he treated them as young children; the memories I have are of a constant conflict between them and the fights which left each of them and all of us, especially Iracy, feeling depleted and silent for days. However, towards Wilson and me he was tender and loving. He was also a very caring grandfather, especially to Cesar's children who lived near him later in his life. I am certain that my brothers will have a different perception of their relationship with Odecio, based on their own individual experiences.

Odecio could not comprehend that the world was changing, that young people were trying hard to liberate themselves from the hypocritical values imposed on them by parents who could not hold it together themselves, by a decaying society led by politicians and military rulers that reinforced law and order through the barrel of a machine gun while helping themselves to the country's coffers. Heathcliff began to spend more and more time with Cesar at the hippy communes around São Paulo.

Wilson was still young but spent a lot of time outside with his friends. He was the most grounded out of all of us. I feel that being the youngest, he soaked up all the influences around him, instinctively embracing the good qualities of his elder brothers and father; he also developed a strong love for literature, philosophy, politics, music, and adopted Odecio's strong work ethic; he decided that alcohol, drugs and the destructive behaviour of the youth he was surrounded by, were definitely not for him.

As we grew up, trying to make sense of our inner and outer worlds, I knew very little of what was going on with my brothers, yet there were still fun moments between us; my brothers shared a wicked sense of humour.

I was also growing up trying to survive and find my purpose among the chaos of my own human mess. In my heart I felt nothing but immense love for my mother, father and brothers. I wanted so much for them. But I did not possess a magical wand. I could only try to love them without judgement. I tried to understand. I am still trying to understand the reasons behind all our behaviours.

At the age of twelve I began to feel out of place everywhere. After school I would rush home. I didn't have many friends and on the rare occasions I was invited back after school by one girl or another, I felt like a fish out of water. Their houses were so rich and tidy compared to mine, the mothers so prim, proper and quiet. More than anything, it was the silence and the formality that I could not stomach. So, I avoided further invitations and was happy to rush home and be with my *Mamae*. I was not pretty or clever or funny or at all interesting, just painfully shy and self-conscious when I was away from home. So, I did not fit in any camp. I began to feel anxious and very alone. The only time I felt fine was when I was with my mother, aunties and my cousins. At my Auntie Lurdes, Orminda and Efigenias' houses I felt that I almost belonged – they were still members of the Assembly of God and I was by then a twelve-year-old sinner, brought up outside of the Church – but I felt loved by them and had a lot of fun with my cousins.

At that time things were difficult at home, money was tight: our rent had gone up, but Odecio's wages had not. I was finding it increasingly difficult dealing with the girls at school and their silly preoccupations about bra sizes, spotty boys and what to wear to the next party. I listened to them absently. I constantly worried about my parents, my brothers and the uncertainty of our lives.

After school I often found Iracy bent over her sewing machine. She no longer created her beautiful inventions or copied designs from fashion magazines but seemed to spend hours repairing clothes for everyone.

'How was school?' She looked up looking intensely at me, 'You know you can bring your schoolmates home; I will bake a *fuba* cake, make some fresh popcorn, fresh sweetcorn on the cob, would you like me to talk to the other mums?'

'No, *Mamae*, it is not like that anymore, the girls act all grown up and make their own arrangements, it is ok you don't have to worry.'

'You seem at a loss these days, of course I worry. I get it, it is a difficult age, the girls around here are a bit young for you now and they go to different schools, and your cousins live far away.'

'And I don't fit in with the girls at school, I don't know what to say to them.'

She continued to give me all her attention. I went on.

'I want to find a job, help at home a bit,' I said and immediately wondered what that was all about. It came from an unknown part of me.

'And your studies?'

'I could go to school in the evenings next year when I turn thirteen.'

'And what kind of work would you do? It will be exhausting working in the day and attending the evening shift at school.'

'I am bored, there is nothing for me to do after school and you don't let me help around the house.'

'I don't want you tied to the kitchen sink like me. If you are serious, then we should try to get you some work in the day after school and if you cope then you can go to the evening school shifts.'

I was over the moon. I felt that my life was about to start. Through word of mouth, she found out that a company selling encyclopedias was offering girls a commission-based opportunity. I was hired immediately. I was picked up at home by a van carrying around ten women from all different backgrounds. Some were housewives looking for extra cash, some were quite old and some in their twenties. The van driver would take us to the new satellite towns spreading on the outskirts of São Paulo. He would carve up the area, park the van in a central place and hand us the encyclopedias. And off we went under the midday sun, knocking on doors trying to convince the residents of the importance of owning those books of knowledge. It became apparent that no one was going to take a skinny, dark and shy girl like me seriously and many doors were slammed in my face. At the end of the shift, we all gathered around the van and reported our sales. Some of the ladies had done well and would receive a pay cheque at the end of the month. We all got back in the van to start the long journey back home. I sat quietly looking out of the window. I felt the world on my shoulders.

'Hey, don't be upset, it takes time. It took me ages to sell my first one, hang in there, the commission is pretty good. No one wants this rotten job,' one of the ladies said trying to comfort me.

They all burst out laughing and so did I.

'I think the encyclopedias are too heavy for her to carry, she is only a kid,' said a much older lady who looked like a grandmother and had a pleasant toothless smile, she went on, 'Have you heard they are launching an encyclopedia for children next month? They may be easier for her to carry.'

This banter went on for a while. They all tried to solve my problems and give me hope. I loved them for that.

When the driver dropped me at home, I gave each of the ladies a hug – a 'thank you for your kindness, thank you for thinking of me' kind of hug. I left the van and walked over to the driver.

'Is there a number I can call to put my name down to sell the children's encyclopedias?'

'Stick with me kid, even if you don't manage to sell anything between now and when the children's stuff comes out, it will be a good experience for you. Maybe you should go with one of the more experienced ladies, they like you, they will teach you a thing or two about selling.'

The matter was settled. I loved being picked up and joining the team. I was part of a team, although not a winning one.

As soon as the children's encyclopedias arrived, the van driver showed them to us. I fell in love with them. There were four small volumes all bound in colourful binders in pale green and yellow. They were light, and much easier to carry. I looked inside and could not stop reading the vast amount of information, all written in such an appealing way, with so many brightly-coloured pictures.

I was so enthusiastic about them that on the first day I managed to sell four sets. My tactic was simple. I knocked on the door and asked if there were any primary school children in the house. When the customer said yes, I would perk up: 'then I came to the right house. I am happy to show you and your children this amazing little encyclopedia, perfectly designed and illustrated to feed young minds.' When I'd grabbed their attention, I went on, 'Let's admit that a child starts school full of enthusiasm just like I did, but their learning must be inspired beyond school.' I would sit on the floor, open the binders and share the contents with the kids in a playful way. It worked every time. That month I sold enough encyclopedias to help a bit at home and buy Wilson his first bicycle. To this day, the feeling of euphoria and pride from my first pay cheque remains the best feeling, despite other achievements that followed.

But the company, which was doing so well selling a range of educational products, went bankrupt. We sold the last items, said our goodbyes and went our separate ways. I was devastated. But soon life went back to the abnormal normality I was accustomed to.

During that time two big events happened that would change me forever.

I remember sitting outside our house one afternoon after school. It had been an uneventful day. Then I saw him. He was walking towards our house. He was an apparition, an alien sight never seen before at Rua Assungui. He wore silky, shiny bell-bottoms with bright orange and yellow

211

psychedelic patterns, a tie-dye T-shirt all the colours of the rainbow, brown messy hair down to his shoulders, rose-tinted sunglasses and the widest grin I had ever seen on anyone's face.

'Hi, is Cesar or Heathcliff in?' I froze on the spot; I could not feel my feet and my mouth went dry. I felt a strange mix of panic, fear and excitement all rolled into one.

'No.' That was all I could manage.

'No? Just, no?' and he laughed and laughed.

'You must be the sister; I am Marius Mancio and this day is getting better by the minute. It is very nice to meet you.'

'And you.'

'And now you are supposed to tell me your name,' he said holding his gaze.

'Walkiria, but everyone calls me Kira and my parents and brothers sometimes call me Kirinha, now my aunties call me Kirinha all the time but if they think I am up to no good or disrespectful of God, you see they are true believers, then they call me Walkiria in a very serious tone.'

I went on and on, talking nonsense, giving too much useless information away and feeling totally stupid at my sudden attack of verbal diarrhea. He stared at me and just laughed. We talked for a while about nothing. Then he took my hand, kissed it, planted a kiss on my cheek and went.

I stood there like a statue, paralysed with that strange panicky feeling mixed with other feelings I could not place, watching the colourful apparition disappear into the distance. When I came to my senses, there was a strange void right in the middle of my being that had not been there before. My mind was filled with images of the weirdest boy I had ever seen. Suddenly, Rua Assungui, the kids playing outside, the mothers gossiping, my house, turned into a hazy shade of dirty grey.

I was brought back to reality by my father's melodic whistling and the smell of his aftershave. He could be heard, and you could smell him, even before he turned the corner of our street.

'Hello *meu, Tesoro* – my treasure – everything all right? You look a bit unwell.'

'Yes, I think it is a bit too hot and I have been doing too much homework.'

'Take it easy, Kirinha, let's go inside and I will make you some fresh lemonade, you could be a bit dehydrated.'

A few days went by, and we met again, this time at a park near his house. I had executed a cunning plan and discovered that he lived near a library in quite a posh area not too far from me.

'*Mamae*, after school, I need to go to the library in Jardim da Saude, I need to find some stuff about a school project.'

Lies, lies, alibis. It was amazing what that strange void right in the middle of my being was capable of orchestrating.

He saw me first. He came rushing in my direction, a swirling magical explosion of colour.

'Hi, Walkiria, it is so good to see you around here. I got the Beatles' *Sgt. Pepper* album, have you heard it? It is the most incredible mixture of sounds I have ever heard. You will not believe what those four have gone and done now; a totally different direction in their music.' He went on and on, so passionate was he about the album.

'Come over to mine, I don't live far, you can listen to it.'

His house was in one of the beautiful suburbs of São Paulo, which felt to me like a different world. Lush ancient trees lined his road, the large houses were of Portuguese colonial style, comprising the two ideals of beauty and function. I had never been inside a house so grand. His mother was called Dona Zantina – meaning the little saint in Spanish. She greeted us warmly. She wore a pair of tiny shorts, and heavy eye make-up. She had a cigarette in one hand and a glass of whisky in the other. I had never seen a mother dress like her or smoke and drink like she did.

'Where is my kiss, Mauriusinho – little Maurius – who is the girl?'

'It is none of your business, Zantina, leave us alone, will you?'

He gave her a hateful look and led me to the basement of the house. The basement was set up for him: a mattress on the floor, the walls covered with posters of the Beatles, The Rolling Stones, Caetano Veloso, Jimi Hendrix, Bob Dylan, Os Mutantes, Janis Joplin and many more rebellious rock stars. He had several electric guitars and Marshall amps. Shelves of records and a few record players. He placed *Sgt. Pepper's* at full volume and sat with his right ear glued to the speakers, shaking his head and trying to sing the melodies, making the sounds of the English words neither *of us could understand.*

Picture yourself in a boat on a river
With tangerine trees and marmalade skies
Somebody calls you, you answer quite slowly
A girl with kaleidoscope eyes

My heart went out to this weird boy who loved the Beatles more than anything else in this world.

Cellophane flowers of yellow and green
Towering over your head
Look for the girl with the sun in her eyes
And she's gone
Lucy in the sky with diamonds
Lucy in the sky with diamonds
Lucy in the sky with diamonds

I looked around his room. He had everything money could buy. Zantina showered him with guitars, electric keyboards and

215

amplifiers, but he could not play any of the expensive instruments lying around. He could pose just like Hendrix but could not play a single note. I thought of Cesar and Wilson who were trying to teach themselves to play guitar with an old, battered acoustic. They were always practicing and learning new chords and arpeggios from books they borrowed from friends, always asking anyone they could to teach them new things on the guitar.

Marius was a serious problem for his mother; to make the problem go way she gave him plenty of money and anything he asked for.

A voice in my head started to tell me to run out of that eerie basement, out of that house, away from that weird boy, away from that creepy mother.

But he came out of his trance, stretched his hand and tried to pull me towards where he was sitting with his head almost inside of the speakers. I shook my head.

'It is too loud for me.'

He got up, turned down the music, walked towards me and looked at me. I could see he had been crying. I had seen that lost, desperate look ever since I could remember in another orphan's eyes. He was silently imploring me to stay, to offer some comfort, some miracle to help him regulate the mumble jumble of twisted emotions going around in his head. So, I did what was by now natural to me: I stayed and tried to offer some comfort.

From that day on, we spent every afternoon after school together. We went to parks, little coffee shops, artisan chocolate shops, ice cream parlours and interesting little boutiques in the best parts of the city. He knew all the best places in São Paulo; he spent Zantina's money on feeding me handmade chocolates, cute little cupcakes and pistachio ice cream with real pistachios all over it. I was impressed with how well received he was by a lot of people that worked in those posh establishments. Little did I know that he was the favourite customer of some very unsavoury drug dealers. But I was in love, the kind of in love that hits you over the head with a hammer and makes you lose all sense of reality. Through my temporary insanity, I could only see a halo above his head and feel his angel wings engulfing me, making everything perfectly vibrant and perfectly perfect. It was us against the world. By now I was fully conversant with the layers and layers of sounds coming out of *Sgt. Pepper's Lonely Hearts Club Band*. We spent hours trying to imagine what all those words meant, making psychedelic assumptions all our own. One afternoon, when I got to his house after school, Dona Zantina greeted me at the gate.

'Hi, I don't even know your name, but he is not here.'

'Oh, he didn't tell me he was going to be out.'

'Come in, I think we need to have a little chat.'

I followed her to the immense lounge; I was surprised how messy it was. Old newspapers, magazines and books covered the floor; an expensive antique wood and metal coffee table was covered with dirty cups and dozens of dirty, half-drunk whisky tumblers. The place had a sour smell of stale cigarettes, booze and disease.

'Whisky?'

'Orange juice, please.'

'Cigarettes? Cannabis?'

'No, thank you.'

'Oh, my oh my, there is so much you don't know about my boy but don't act all innocent with me, I know you kids do a lot of drugs.'

If at first, I disliked this pompous, entitled, arrogant woman, now I hated her.

'He is very unwell. He is under a psychiatrist. He has outbursts of uncontrollable anger. He has even tried to kill his uncle.'

This was too much for my young, madly-in-love heart to bear. I was paralysed by fear, by anger, by a desperate need to take him away from that dark, ugly house, from that woman whose stale nicotine breath was making me feel nauseous.

'I can tell you love him; I think we will have to work together to keep him safe. He will be spending a couple days at a psychiatric centre where they will try different medication;

the nurses will monitor his reaction. When he comes out, he will be on the recommended drugs for the foreseeable future.'

'But what can I do?' I did not recognise the sound of my own voice when it finally came out. It sounded weak, nervous and tremulous.

'Just keep him away from recreational drugs, or any drugs. You must stop him from meeting the people who give him drugs.'

I nodded. It hurt even to nod my head. I felt a heaviness coming down on me from the top of my head all the way down to my toes. I could not feel my body, I felt the room growing dark and Zantina's voice growing distant.

'He will be like a loose cannon if he mixes the prescribed psychiatric drugs with all the junk he takes.'

I could tell she was getting a little tipsy. I got up to go home.

'I will try my best, I want him to be well.'

'Now that's a good girl. You never know if you manage to keep him in check, you guys may even marry, he is already the owner of several flats in the centre of São Paulo, you know.'

And here I was, right in the middle of a drama that was too heavy for me to carry and too complex for me to begin to understand. My heart went out to him. I liked the idea of taking care of him and even the possibility of marrying him. The fact that I was fourteen and he was seventeen did not cross my mind.

When I got home, Iracy was waiting for me outside.

'How was the library? You must have been studying a lot and reading some pretty sad stories by the look on your face, Kirinha.'

I nodded and said nothing. I had not learnt the art of burying everything inside, of placing a smile on my face, of carrying on singing little tunes to cover up my feelings and situations. I was mad at her interference.

'I know you have not been going to the library, unless Marius' house is now the library.'

I was shocked; she'd had me followed. I was outraged. I did not need this, not now.

'*Mamae*,' I said angrily, 'we are going steady, and we really love each other, we may marry.'

She nodded and what felt like an eternity passed before she spoke again.

'Very few girls will escape what you are going through my daughter. It is nature. But I am telling you now, whatever you do, don't get pregnant, there is no need for that. If you do, there are ways of not being pregnant, also, this generation's poison does not seem to be alcohol but drugs – destructive demons I have never heard of before. Be careful, be alert, only you can protect yourself from now on. All I can do is to pick up the pieces. I will pick them up with you, always. You don't have to fear me, no matter what I say, how I say it, remember I am on your side.'

Looking back on this advice, which confused me at the time, I now feel blessed to have had a forward-thinking mother who liberated me from a set of patriarchal Christian values that have been annihilating women's choices and independence for centuries. A wonderful legacy to pass on to my daughter and my son.

Trying hard to hide my tears, I ran inside. She knew everything. I felt exposed and foolish, but I knew she had left a window open for me to come back in.

I didn't go back to meet him at his house. I was overwhelmed by what Zantina had told me. I just waited, perplexed, hoping and praying just like my aunties and my cousins did, for him to come to me.

The following Saturday my prayers were answered, and he came to our house. He seemed a little sedated as if he was struggling to keep awake; his vibrant personality was gone, replaced by a vacant look. We hugged, I cried.

'That bitch gave you her little speech about me, didn't she?'

'She told me about your uncontrollable outbursts of anger, Marius.'

He must have noticed the fear in my eyes.

'I would never, I mean never, hurt you, but if I could, I would murder her and him!'

'Who is he? And why do you hate her so much?'

221

He told me in his sedated state that from the age of ten he had witnessed his father's cancer take away his vitality and, finally, his will to live. He reminisced how much he loved his father. He had fond memories of his father taking care of him, taking him to the park to fly kites, to play football. These moments were the happiest of his life. Zantina was often absent, taking care of business, but even when she was around, she was somehow even more absent and never joined them in their games, outings or activities.

We sat in silence for a long time.

'But it wasn't her fault he developed cancer, Marius.'

'Did you know that emotional stress can cause cancer?'

'No way! Who told you that?'

'I heard my grandmother – my father's mother – saying this to some of my father's uncles and aunties when he became so ill that a hospital bed and a nurse arrived at our house. He was placed in the spare room, next to the master room.'

'Why was he under emotional stress?'

'I don't really know when it started. Ever since I can remember that piece of shit has always been hanging around our house like a bad smell.'

'Who?'

'My father's younger brother. The portfolio of properties and other businesses are family-owned so him and my father worked together taking care of everything. They were very close until Zantina started to find every excuse to be alone with Uncle. It was so obvious they were at it all the time. My elder brother left home to attend medical school and I was left right in the middle of that sick incestuous triangle. The fights were endless, with Zantina and Dad screaming insults at each other at the top of their voices. Things got so bad I asked to move to the basement.'

I sat there next to him, holding his hand, trying to create a safe space for his story to unfold.

'But it was two against one and my dad was asked to leave. He wouldn't', he couldn't'. He stayed because of me. I heard him shouting at them both once. "I will get out of your way when my job as a father is done. When he leaves for university or to take care of his life, I will get out of your lives for good. In the meantime, I am not going anywhere, I will continue to take care of him like I always did." A few months later he was diagnosed with terminal cancer. The rest is history. At his funeral, I could not move away from his grave. I just stood there. It was then that I started hearing voices. So many voices in my head, some laughing at me, some mocking me and my dad. When I looked around, I saw her and that piece of shit walking away holding hands.'

We sat in silence on the floor, outside my tiny house at Rua Assungui, without realising it had become dark and the

223

streetlights were on and the night bugs were already flying around, buzzing their annoying sounds, doing whatever night bugs did. At that moment I wished I was a firefly glowing in the dark throwing some light on the darkness that had descended on the love of my life, my future husband and I.

He went home, I went in, sat in the lounge with my parents and watched some soap opera. I felt safe inside. Iracy had just baked a *fuba* cake. It was as if she knew instinctively that I needed her *fuba* cake love.

I was no longer allowed to go to the library after school; her spies were everywhere. But she was ok with him coming to our house. He seemed to like coming to us. He ate whatever was on offer. Iracy was surprised at how such a rich boy could be so famished all the time.

'Don't they feed him at home?' She would enquire later.

Things took a turn for the worse. He met me outside my school one afternoon. His speech was slurred, his eyes glazed, and he was not making any sense at all.

'Shall we call your mum?'

'No, come with me to my brother's flat in town, his wife will be there, we can take a cab.'

We arrived in no time at all at a very modern residential block with a security guard at the front. He knew Marius and let us in straight away. His sister-in-law let us in. By then Marius was struggling to put one foot in front of the other. He lay on top of the rug in the lounge and went straight off to sleep. We left him there, while she made coffee, and we sat in the lounge chatting about that crazy family. She told me she had just recently married his brother. Zantina had given them a generous living allowance and the flat. They opted for a minimalistic look. They had hardly any furniture, a few pieces of novel art pieces made their apartment look like an art exhibition. She was an artist in her last year of art school. We were worlds apart.

'I would stay away from Zantina if I were you. She has the talent for entering your mind — without you even noticing — and poisoning it. We survive by avoiding her.'

A few hours went by, it was getting late, and I needed to go home. I called Marius, shook his head from side to side, but he was dead the world.

We carried on sitting next to him and chatting. His brother arrived and took one look at the scene in his front room, hurried over to his brother, examined his eyes and shouted, 'Call an ambulance, he is in a coma, you stupid girls, how could you not have noticed he was intoxicated.' The ambulance came in no time at all – one of the perks of expensive private healthcare – and took him away. I started to cry hysterically.

'Calm down, we don't need this right now, just tell me what he has been taking.'

'I have no idea, he met me at the school gates. He was already slurring his speech and his movements were slow, too slow. He got us in a taxi, and we arrived here.'

Marius had taken the whole bottle of medication. His brother had arrived just in time to save his life. He spent a couple of days in A&E and was then transferred to a psychiatric hospital in rural São Paulo.

Iracy kept her promise and tried hard to pick up the pieces of my broken heart. She never said much, just listened, made sure I ate and offered distraction. She talked incessantly about what was happening with all our relatives. Some stories were tragic and made me cry even more, so she changed and shared my cousins' more humorous shenanigans that made me laugh with her. In her typically secretive manner, she found out where Marius was hospitalised and took a coach at the crack of dawn, before any of us were up, telling Odecio she had an early medical appointment. Upon her return, she shared her visit with me. She told me she had seen him and that he was responding to treatment. She convinced the psychiatrist in charge of him to see her. She wanted to find out what was wrong with him. She wanted to know the real facts, not all the assumptions everyone was making. She sat with me and shared the conversation she had with the psychiatrist.

'Marius is a very disturbed young man, he has been hearing voices since his father passed away. His home environment, how can I put it, it is not helping his recovery.'

'But what is wrong with him exactly?'

'He is schizophrenic, Dona Iracy, his condition can be controlled with medication and regular visits to a psychiatrist, however, he also needs a lot of support at home.'

'It is going to take a lot of love.'

'Yes, beautifully put Dona Iracy.'

'*Mamae*, I have all the love in the world for him, I am sure I can help him get better.'

She didn't argue. She was wise enough to know that there was nothing that she could say that would change my feelings overnight.

'Time, Kirinha, time will tell whether your love will be enough. Sometimes not even love is enough, but only life can teach you that.'

Maurius came out of hospital after six weeks or so. He came straight to our house. As I write, I struggle to describe the feeling of relief, euphoria and infinite possibilities I felt for that broken boy. At that time, I was convinced that our love could endure and conquer anything. He seemed changed, more subdued. We hugged, kissed a lot and cried a lot. A few days later, he met me again after school. I remember it was a Friday. He told me he was going to say a quick hello to a friend he had met at the hospital who was a constant companion. This friend supported Marius when he was in and out of deep sleep therapy, pumped with barbiturates. This barbaric psychiatric treatment was still being used in Brazil. All sorts of treatments could be given while the patient was kept sleeping, including a variety of drugs and ECT which caused considerable memory loss.

We took a taxi to the centre of town and soon arrived at his friend's building. He asked me to wait in the lobby saying he was not going to be long. I stood there certain that something was terribly wrong. When he came down, he was already altered, gone was the subdued manner, instead he was agitated, his eyes shone.

'Ahhh, it is great to feel alive again, they are all trying to fuck with my brains, take my mind away. But I know them, I know their tricks.'

I was petrified. He seemed to have gone over the edge in less than an hour. I knew he had taken some sort of hallucinogenic drug by the way he was speaking. That person next to me, walking fast, spitting dozens of incomprehensible words at me, was a stranger and a very dangerous one at that.

'What they don't know, Walkiria, is that I am stronger, far more intelligent than all of them put together. I am God-like, and I can fly.'

'Marius, I want to go home,' I almost whispered.

'Please don't tell me you are going to run home and tell her, warn her and that piece of shit before I get to them, tell me you are on my side, TELL ME!!'

228

He was yelling right in my face. He grabbed me by the hair and punched my mouth. I started to bleed. A strange feeling of calmness engulfed every cell of my body and every corner of my mind; I gently pushed him away, looked, unafraid, into his eyes. I could taste the blood inside of my mouth.

'I would never run out on you. You are stronger and more intelligent than any of them. You are a God, and they need to know that.'

He gave out a menacing laugh and kissed me.

'I feel so powerful, I know I can fly.' He was walking fast again, towards a bridge or a viaduct just behind Avenida Paulista. He climbed on the edge of the bridge and looked down at all the cars going fast below him.

'Nothing can touch us, come hold my hand, let's fly, let's prove to everyone what we can do.'

I was still engulfed by that peaceful feeling. I felt very grounded. I felt as if there was someone else there with me; my mind felt sharp, resolved to escape that nightmare.

'My beautiful, powerful God,' I was surprised at the cold stillness of my own voice. 'Let me watch you fly first in all your glory, then come and get me and teach me how to fly.'

He smiled at me, opened his arms, turned his head up to the sky and let out a loud scream at the top of his voice.

That was the moment I needed to run away from him. I ran like I had never run before. I kept breathing in and out, trying not to run out of breath, running for my life as fast as I could until I got back to the avenue. The traffic lights were red, and I banged on the first car window I saw.

'Please help me, I have been attacked, there is a madman after me.'

I will never forget the face of the young man who opened his car door to me.

'Where do you need to go?'

'Rua Assungui, near Jardim da Saude.'

'Is your mother or your father there to receive you?'

'Yes.'

'Promise me you will be safe there.'

'I promise.'

'There is some water in the glove compartment and some tissues. Try and stay calm, drink the water and clean the blood from your mouth. Now take a deep breath, hold it in and let it go slowly.' He made me repeat this several times as he drove away from Avenida Paulista. 'I had this feeling all day that I didn't want to go to Uni tonight anyway.'

He was a medical student. He worked all day to pay for his studies, doing whatever jobs he could and was trying hard to finish his medical training.

I told him the full story. He shared with me the many casualties he saw due to this new hallucinogenic drug that had arrived in Brazil called LSD. He said that Marius had probably been given a bad batch. He also said that LSD and a cocktail of psychiatric drugs may have caused a psychotic episode.

'LSD,' I repeated out loud.

'Lucy in the Sky with Diamonds,' he replied.

'Like in the song?'

'Yeah! Do you know the song? One of my favourites.'

'I must have heard it a thousand times, but I have no idea what it means.'

He translated it for me. He knew English. He was very educated and, on his way, to becoming a doctor. But somewhere along his upbringing someone had helped him educate his heart too. What a powerful combination, I thought, an educated mind and a heart full of kindness.

How I wished I could have been that girl with kaleidoscope eyes, living in a world with tangerine trees and marmalade skies. How mind-blowing, the fact that although Marius did not know what the lyrics of his favourite song meant, he tried to live in a psychedelic world and even wore the colours depicted in 'Lucy in the Sky with Diamonds'; how bizarre that what had finally tipped him over the edge was again his Lucy in the Sky with Diamonds.

Picture yourself in a boat on a river

With tangerine trees and marmalade skies

Somebody calls you, you answer quite slowly

A girl with kaleidoscope eyes

231

We soon got to Rua Assungui. I thanked him profusely.

'I will never be able to repay you for saving my life tonight. I know you will be the finest of doctors and save many lives.'

'That's the dream, and I hope yours comes true too.'

I went into my house, thinking that I no longer had any dreams; it was late, past 9pm. I had never stayed out this late before. Iracy and Odecio were sitting in the kitchen in silence looking forlorn and drinking *cafezinhos*.

'Where have you been?' What happened to your mouth?' They both shouted almost in unison.

I told my own version of the story. I was economical with the truth about my cut lip, telling them I had fallen while trying to run. I left out the part where I told him to fly on his own. I was still thrown off balance by the night's events. I felt totally conflicted. I kept repeating in my head again and again: how could I have manipulated his mind to save my own skin? How could I have told him to fly alone, basically encouraging him, this sick boy I was meant to love, to jump off a viaduct? Had he jumped? Was he dead by now? I could almost hear the sirens. I pictured the police and ambulances arriving at the scene. Marius smashed on the floor, blood everywhere. A tiny and insane part of my awareness wished that he had superpowers and really could fly. I did not want him dead.

What had happened to all that love I felt for him just a few hours before? Is anyone capable of loving, or turning the other cheek, when their survival is at stake? As much as I would like to fantasize that we are here to love one another, the crude reality is that we are here to survive; but love can and will always flourish when we learn to survive by caring equally for each other. It became clear to me that this was never the case with Marius and me.

Odecio became tearful, looking at my bruised fat lip, listening to my state of turmoil.

'Swear to me he did not hit you; you are my little girl, I am supposed to protect you.'

I hated to see him in this way.

'*Papai*, please don't start blaming yourself, I am to blame, no one else.'

'No one is to blame, no one knew how disturbed the boy was, none of us saw it coming and I bet we have not heard the last of it.'

As *Mamae* spoke her wise words, we heard someone shouting outside. It was Zantina with Marius' uncle.

'He hasn't returned home, and his medicine makes him very sleepy, he knows he should be home by seven at the very latest.'

She was a sight in her hot pants, with her blue eyeshadow, slurring her words with a fag in her hand. The sight of her was too much for me to bear; the events of the night, combined with the control I had to exercise to flee to safety, the fear that he had jumped and the corrosive guilt eating at my insides, came crushing down on me and opened the floodgates. I began to shake and cry convulsively. Iracy took me indoors and made a huge glass of water with five spoons of sugar and some red wine.

'Sit down, drink this slowly, let your father handle the situation,' Odecio came back in.

'I told them the whole story. I let them know roughly where you think you left him. I am going with them to look for him.'

I stayed behind with *Mamae*. The concoction she made me calmed me down and I felt sleepy.

Odecio came back in the early hours. It transpired that he was alive and in prison. He had not jumped. He carried on running around and shouting about being God, and he tried to attack a group of students who called the police and had him arrested. He was put behind bars. At Odecio's suggestion they searched the hospitals close to the area and then the police stations. He was in a complete psychotic state and was to be transferred to a psychiatric hospital first thing in the morning. Zantina begged my father to let me go in the ambulance with him. He had been calling for me all night.

'Only if she wants to and if I come with her.'

She had asked her older son to come as well. So, the next morning, Odecio, Marius' brother and I jumped in the ambulance, collected him from the police station and took him back to the psychiatric hospital he'd left just a couple of months before.

Throughout the journey, his brother engaged his psychotic fantasies, agreeing with him, making very convincing arguments about the power of the mind, telling him that his mind had reached a state of evolution which made him superior to others and that he was being taken to a special centre where his mind was going to be studied and analysed. My father – the Daddy Bear – sat between me and Marius, in case he tried to hurt me in any way. Marius felt safe in his brother's presence and in his description of his superior mind. My presence also soothed him; he kept looking at me with loving eyes and smiling. I tried hard but failed to hold in the tears that kept running down my cheeks all the way there. When we got there four strong male nurses were already waiting. When he saw them, he panicked and froze on the spot.

'No!' he screamed, 'you all lied to me, you don't believe a word of what I have been telling you, you betrayed me, you betrayed me!!'

They took him by force and strapped him to a stretcher and took him away. I could hear his screams echoing in my head as we jumped in Zantina's car. She had been following the ambulance. He was to be sectioned indefinitely in the high-risk wing of the psychiatric hospital. No visitors were allowed for the foreseeable future.

I cried all the way home, I cried the rest of that night, I cried the next day and the days following. My love for him had returned tenfold.

'*Mamae*, I will never see him again. I can't see the point of going on living.'

I stopped eating.

She said nothing, just agreed with me that life was too much for us to bear at times. She just insisted I drank water and made me soup. She respected my need to grieve and left me alone. After a few weeks, she encouraged me to try and do my grieving at this club we had frequented some years back. She encouraged me to grieve by the pool. At first, I hesitated. When we frequented that club as children, Wilson was found at the bottom of the adult swimming pool. No one knew how long he had been there or exactly what had happened to him on that day. He was a good swimmer. His salvation was the fact that right opposite the club there was a hospital. He stayed hospitalised for a long time. It was touch and go. I remember visiting him with my parents and brothers every day. Everyone at the Assembly of God dedicated entire services and prayers for him. During the weeks he was hospitalised I prayed with all my strength to

God, as he was known by my aunties. I prayed to all the saints known to the Catholic Church, I prayed to all the African and the ancient Tupi-Guarani Goddesses too. He came to after what seemed an eternity. At first, he could not recognise anyone, but then he was as good as new and we took our baby home with us. My parents, brothers and I were giddy with happiness and relief. Despite my reservations of going back to that club, Iracy had a cunning way of agreeing and empathising with your concerns and then, as if by magic, making you do exactly what she wanted you to do in the first place.

She bought me my first grown-up bikini. It was white with some specks of black making a pretty pattern. She helped me pack a bag with some teen magazines, gave me some money for the fare and put me on the bus. I began to enjoy my grieving at the club, under the hot sun, jumping in the pool to cool down. One day this beautiful boy came to talk to me. He was tanned, with perfect white teeth – he was funny, untroubled and talked about his loving family. He sat next to me most days I was there. I could not have imagined that grieving could feel that good. But when he invited me to his house to meet his mother, I told him where to go and ran a mile. But I continued to enjoy my grieving at the club until it was time to return to school.

Iracy was a total and utter emotionally intelligent genius.

Life is a borrowed gift and must go on

Life went on. I went back to school. I was much changed and so were the girls in my class. Some had dealt with broken hearts, some had to deal with abortions, some were absent due to pregnancies, some were coming to terms with their parent's divorces, some were taking drugs, and some were confused about their sexuality. At the end of the first week, I went straight to the headmistress and asked to be transferred to the night school.

I needed a fresh start. At night school the students were treated with so much more respect. They varied in age and were from similar backgrounds. No one wore hideous uniforms. All we had to do was to wear a white apron on top of our clothes during school hours. All of them worked. There was room to be more autonomous. For the first time I felt part of something. For an art project, I motivated some colleagues to put on a play. I wrote the idea of the play – a family from the north-east of Brazil leaving everything behind to find work in São Paulo – the group's creativity flowed from the idea, and we put on the play. My parents and brothers attended the opening. The play was very well received by the school. We got to stage it at various schools in São Paulo.

Through a schoolmate, I got a full-time job as a receptionist at a law firm in the centre of São Paulo. I found it difficult at first but soon fell into a routine. Straight from work I went to night school. I had boundless energy. I was growing up fast and I got on well with my schoolmates, who were a lot older than me.

It was during that time that I met Jojo – Jose Antonio. I used to go past his house after school to catch the bus. He always stood in front of his house and smiled at me. I never smiled back. One day I was walking with some school friends who happened to know him, and we were formally introduced. We started to talk and became friends. He was mature, gentle and grounded. I really liked talking to him. He was surprised that I was only fifteen and I was surprised that he was already nearly twenty-five. We started to hang out but there was nothing serious between us. He came to my house and met everyone. He was shy and Odecio tormented him mercilessly with his jokes and concerns. Life was running smoothly again.

Then the day we all dreaded finally came. The owner of our house in the middle of our street – Rua Assungui – announced that he was selling his properties to a new developer and asked us to vacate the house. My parents put up a good fight to stay but to no avail. All I know was that legal eviction papers had been issued; we ran the risk of being homeless if we did not find another house fast.

As I left for work one morning, Iracy asked me for my work number. She told me not to worry and that she would call me and give me the new address. Although I was anxious for all of us, the way she reassured me made me trust that if anyone could do the impossible, and even perform a miracle, it was her.

Little did we know that behind-the-scenes Iracy was in negotiations with a government housing scheme that helped working families to buy their own home. The process was well underway and even the house to be purchased had been chosen by her; the only thing missing was a sponsor. What I also didn't know was that the polite conversations she seemed to be having with Jojo when he came to our house was also part of her plan. She learnt from Jojo that his brother and mother were professionals with reasonable incomes; without even talking to me, she marched to Jojo's house, introduced herself and asked the impossible of those strangers. To this day I do not know how she convinced them to buy a house with her so that we would not be homeless. I cannot even begin to describe my embarrassment; I wanted to be swallowed by the ground and never be seen again.

Her cunning plot worked. She bought a house in Sao Bernardo dos Campos, a small town that was still part of the Metropolitan region of Sao Paulo.

Soon after, she could free Jojo's brother from the deeds of the house and any further liability.

But that was the way she operated: always secretly, in mysterious ways, waving her magic wand and saving us all.

The house was such a step up for us. There were three bedrooms, a large kitchen-diner, a lovely lounge and a laundry area. It was brand new. For the very first time in my life, I had my own bedroom. I no longer needed to sleep in the lounge, sharing the sofa bed with Wilson.

The second event that would change my life forever happened on the 1st of February 1974.

We were now living in São Bernado dos Campos in our brand-new house. The commute was tough. I got up at six in the morning to get into the centre of São Paulo and walk a few blocks to the offices where I worked as a receptionist. But on that day the traffic was at a total standstill: the military police were ordering the bus drivers to let the passengers out, advising them to make the rest of the way on foot. I got out of the bus and started to walk. When I turned into Avenida 9 de Julio, I could see a fire starting at around the tenth floor of the Joelma building; commuters stood by talking among themselves.

'Where is the fire brigade?'

'They will be here in no time at all, the fire is only on one floor, I am sure everyone will be safe.'

I walked fast towards the building where I worked, which was in front of the Joelma building. I did not want to be late. The young secretary, and lover of the senior partner, thirty years her senior, was very pedantic and loved her pep talk every time I was even five minutes late. By the time I reached the office on the fifteenth floor, there was a commotion of partners, junior lawyers, secretaries, junior clerks, tea ladies and even the cleaners, all gathered in the senior partner's large office which had panoramic windows right in front of Joelma's building. At first, I wondered why everyone was gathering there in silence – you could not hear a pindrop. The small fire I had seen only fifteen minutes before was now engulfing the entire building. There were hundreds of people holding onto their lives, standing on the narrow window ledges. As the fire mercilessly engulfed them, many jumped to their deaths.

An air-conditioning unit on the twelfth floor overheated, starting a fire. There were 756 people in the building at the time. Because flammable materials had been used to furnish the interior, the entire building was engulfed in flames within twenty minutes. The fire was extinguished at 1:30 pm, with 179 deaths and 300 people injured.

This happened less than two years after another deadly fire in downtown São Paulo, that of the Andraus Building. As of December 2015, the Joelma fire remains the third-worst skyscraper fire ever in terms of the death toll, after the collapse of the World Trade Centre Twin Towers in New York City on September 11, 2001.

We just stood there. I will never forget the eerie silence in that room where we stood watching in horror as so many men and women, just like us, burnt to death or jumped to their deaths. Even the tears running down our faces were deadly silent.

Jojo came to meet me after work. We went into a coffee shop where many people had gathered, some were sharing the atrocities already published in the evening news. Horror stories with gruesome details of how those poor souls had died and the loved ones they left behind. Very little was published in the media about the people responsible for the fire, how the fire regulations were overlooked or what safety measures were planned to keep the other buildings safe.

Not a word was said between Jojo and me. We both felt that words meant nothing and that it was better to stay in silence. In my silence I realised that what I did for a job meant nothing, nor did my studies or my grueling schedule to make something of myself. Everything that I did, everything that I was had suddenly lost all meaning. There was now just an even bigger pulsating void right in the middle of my being – my very own hungry ghost.

I got home, Iracy was waiting. She had phoned the office, and she knew I was safe. Jojo's mother had managed to reach my mother and told her that he was going to meet me and bring me straight home. This was the beginning of a long friendship between those two mothers.

Intuitively she knew that silence was what I needed. She warmed up some dinner for me and got the *fuba* cake out. I did not touch the dinner but demolished what was left of the cake in one go.

I could not sleep. Around four in the morning I went downstairs. Odecio was already there brewing some fresh coffee. Iracy could not sleep either and joined us.

'I am not sure how I will manage to go back to work, to walk past the burnt building as if nothing has happened.'

'Then don't go back,' they both said almost in unison.

'But what will I do?'

'You have experience in sales, remember how well you were doing?' Odecio said.

'So far you have proven to yourself that you are good at sales, and you are extremely good with children. Look how you have all the small kids following you around and how you enjoy singing to them, making up stories that inspire their imagination,' Iracy was excited, offering me some possibilities.

'Yes,' said Odecio, smiling, 'you are like the Pied Piper of Hamelin.'

'Who the hell is this Pied Piper of Hamelin?' I asked.

We saw the daybreak and the sunlight coming through our kitchen window as Odecio animatedly shared the fable of the Pied Piper of Hamelin. Iracy and I loved the fable.

'Kirinha, go back to bed, I will tell your boss you are too traumatised to go in and I am keeping you at home for a few days. No one can argue with that.'

I obeyed. She looked at me. 'Try and remember that life is a borrowed gift, and it must go on.'

I slept for an eternity, dreaming dreams of the Pied Piper of Hamelin, of a girl with kaleidoscope eyes under tangerine skies and nightmares of a burning house where *Mamae*, *Papai*, my beautiful brothers and amazing little aunties were inside, with me on the outside, desperately trying to save them.

I woke up with my parents' words echoing in my head; I had a talent to sell and I loved children. Through the grapevine I heard of a cosmetics company called Avon that was hiring girls to sell their cosmetics to relatives and friends. They could also sell door-to-door if they wished. I soon found the Avon representative in my area; after a brief training session on the products, I was given a bag containing various samples, colour charts, brochures and promotional leaflets. I became an Avon girl. The fact that I did not wear any make-up or nail polish and went around wearing a pair of jeans, sandals and a simple T-shirt did not dissuade me. Nor did the fact that I could not sell to family members as none of my aunties or cousins – devoted members of the Assembly of God – could wear make-up.

I knocked on doors and often I was welcome by housewives, their teenage daughters and cute grannies who were curious about the products. Some were lonely or bored and invited me in to have a *cafezinho* with them. I sold well, kept the books straight, and helped at home a little. While all this was happening, a desire was growing in me to work with children.

One day I got up early, barely ate my breakfast, picked up my Avon bag, my school bag and armed with that fire in my belly went to make enquiries at the nursery schools near my school. After many frustrating attempts I arrived at a nursery school called Don Patricio, catering for toddlers aged two to four. I made enquiries at the reception. One of the nursery nannies was called to talk to me. She was in her twenties and very sweet.

'Oh, we don't have an opening right now, the owner is tight and focuses a lot on her other school catering for mentally challenged kids, though we could do with an extra pair of hands, especially today, kind of right now. It is

'Parents Inspection Day' and the kids are playing up something terrible and it is only me and Magali for nearly twenty toddlers.' She seemed so stressed, words tumbling out of her mouth 'and we must prepare a file for each child with all their artwork and reports on how they have been behaving and how they are eating or not eating; we have most of the records, but it is all a bit messy and ...' She went on and on.

'I am not doing anything, I can help if you want, it will give me some experience.'

She was over the moon.

'That would be great! Only for a couple of hours to keep an eye on them in the playground.'

The sight of the toddlers playing in the playground took my breath away. They were all different shapes and sizes; I felt I was entering an enchanted world of colour and fun. I observed the rainbow-like spectrum of skin and hair colour and the colourful little outfits they were wearing. Some were happily playing in the sand, some were pushing others around or pulling their hair, some were crying, some were comforting those who were crying, some were running around, some were laughing, some were shyly or perhaps solitarily playing with the toys lying around. I could feel a kind of transcendental energy just watching them. They were all incredibly beautiful, pure and worthy of so much love. To me it was so blissful the fact that they did not yet know how their lives would turn out and how much pain there was in this world, however they also reminded me that despite everything there was a magical wonder that existed in children and in all living things if we looked closely enough. I started by picking up those who were crying or being pushed around and sat with them on the floor; they stared at me; I started singing and making gestures with my hands and giving them encouragement through stupid over-the-top facial expressions; they stared at me as if I was a bit deranged then slowly started to join in.

> *'Ten little monkeys jumping on the bed*
> *one fell out and hit his head*
> *Mama called the doctor and the doctor said*

> *no more monkeys jumping on the bed.'*

Then, one by one, they left whatever they were doing and sat on the floor joining in the fun, singing, making gestures and laughing at the little monkeys falling off the bed.

I don't how long we all stayed there, but being with them made me feel that I was exactly where I should be. Little did I know that the toddlers and I were being watched by the owner of the school and the mothers that were arriving for the inspection day.

I was offered a job but only part-time as they could not afford to pay me full-time wages.

Once again, I had a full life and was enjoying it so much more this time. I got up at 6.30 am and left the house with my father who would drive me to Don Patricio on his way to work – no matter how exhausted I sometimes felt, the little cheeky monkeys at Don Patricio would lift my spirits no end. After my shift ended, I knocked on doors selling Avon and, in the evenings, I would go to school.

It was during this time that I decided to change certain patterns at home: I started celebrating everyone's birthday. I remember buying *Mamae* simple gifts like a pot plant or a beautiful blouse. The night before her birthday I would arrive from night school and clean and tidy the mess left behind, so that she would find her kitchen spotless on the morning of her birthday. I would put flowers in the middle of the table with a card filled with so many fluffy words of love, admiration and gratitude. I would get everyone to sign it. As soon she came to wake me up, I would jump out of bed and give her a massive, big hug wishing her a happy birthday. She blushed a little with embarrassment, feeling a little awkward with my display of affection.

It was also during that time that I made a very serious decision on nothing but gutfeel and impulse. The owner of Don Patricio came in to see us; she was agitated and shared that she desperately needed one of the nursery nannies to help her at her other school for mentally challenged children. Both specialised teachers had come down with flu, and she could not manage on her own. I noticed that no one volunteered, they just looked awkwardly at the floor.

'I don't have any experience or training to deal with such kids – the words she used would be very offensive for me to relate here - and I heard they can be violent,' said one of them.

'We are in the middle of organising the Christmas party and it will take a long time to get the toddlers to learn the song we chose for the day,' said the other.

I was horrified at their attitude towards the mentally challenged children. I felt their prejudice and total disregard for their plight.

'I will do it!'

The owner of the school looked at me. She was of European descent, very well-dressed with a commanding and efficient air.

'Thank you. I really mean it. We will do it together.'

When I entered Don Patricio for Mentally Challenged Children I was confronted with a scene that was very different from the colourful, playful and wondrous playground filled with toddlers. Here there were no giggly sounds of children playing, but a disturbing silence, occasionally interrupted by grunts or sudden screaming. The school was drab, joyless and depressing. There were fifteen kids. As I write I vividly remember a little girl aged twelve – I say a little girl because her mental age was about three or four – called Vanuza. She wore thick pink glasses, a pink dress, pink socks – she was going through her pink phase but, in her case, it was lasting a long time indeed. What struck me most about her was how her eyes looked directly at you through her thick glasses. She had a habit of staring into your eyes with such despair trying to communicate. She could speak in an almost undecipherable language made of normal words one could understand and sounds she made up along the way. When she got frustrated, she would scream, use expletives and bite her right hand with all her might. Her right hand was full of thick, ugly calluses that continuously bled as a testimony of how she felt inside at times. She was not that different from me in her frustration. I also wished I could scream, swear and bite my hand at the many things I had already witnessed.

The first few days were spent learning a bit about each child and trying to ensure some sort of order in their routine. They had all been diagnosed and labelled with one form of autism or another. Little was known in the 1970s in Brazil about autism spectrum disorder. I disliked the way they were referred to as if they were nothing or felt nothing. So, I interacted with them in the same way I did with the toddlers, noticing them, paying attention when they were trying to communicate, giving them the time they needed when they tried to reach out in their own individual ways. I started to discover not only their difficulties but also their personalities, the little things that made them smile and the things that upset them. My heart went out not only to them but to their parents.

I took to the job well and was offered a permanent part-time position. The months rolled on and, in my naivety, I assumed a Christmas party was also being arranged for them.

'I am so excited about the Christmas party for the kids here. What can I do to help.'

'What, are you crazy? We don't do anything for them.'

'But why not?'

'Between you and I, it is not worth it, they have no idea about anything, it would be chaos,' said the main teacher.

Disappointed, I left at the end of that morning. I went about my day making some deliveries to my loyal Avon customers and then going to school at night. I could not stop thinking about the kids and how unfairly they were treated. I could see and sense that they were much more capable than they were credited with. I missed Iracy at times like this. I hardly saw her in those days. By the time I came home, it was nearly midnight, and she was already in bed. But she always kept my dinner warm in the oven.

At the weekend I shared the whole story with her. She went very quiet for a while then started sharing what was on her mind.

'I knew there was something wrong with your cousin Marcus before he was one. But I also felt and observed that although he would

252

struggle to learn he was not much different from other children inasmuch that he needed a bit of structure and a lot of tender loving care to achieve his potential, whatever that might be. My brother Sebastiao asked me to keep an eye and a heart out for him before he passed away; I have been doing this ever since. Marcus is fine, has a happy life, enjoys going to church and feels protected by his mother, myself and all the other family around him.'

I was comforted by her words and motivated to do my best work with the kids at Don Patricio.

The next Monday morning I arrived at Don Patricio full of energy and hope, with a huge grin on my face. It was late November and I had been singing a beautiful Christmas song used in Banco Real's Christmas advert; the melody was as catchy as a nursery rhyme, the lyrics were simple but conveyed a lovely message about hope triumphing over adversity.

As I went about my routine quietly singing the song, I noticed Vanuza staring at me intently with a little smile on her face, moving her head from side to side. I sat next to her and started to sing the song to her. To my surprise she started making the tune and even using some of the words. One by one the other children joined me. After a while we were all singing the hopeful Christmas song the best way we could.

We all felt so elated to see them concentrating, singing and enjoying themselves as a group.

'We could get them to sing this song to the parents and throw a little party, what do you think?' I urged the teachers.

'Maybe we could get away with it, let's get them to sing the song for a few days. We can show the owner and see what she thinks of your idea, Walkiria.'

A week later we gathered the children and called the owner. The teachers, the assistants and I all sang with the children, who took part in their own individual ways, making whatever sound they could and singing the words they could master. The owner was speechless, open-mouthed, shaking her head from side to side. I suggested we set a date, ask the parents to dress the children in red for the day and bring a plate of party food.

There was a new benign energy among us. We all decorated the school with Christmas themes on the day. We dressed in red too.

The image of the children arriving with their parents on the day of the first Christmas school party they ever had is imprinted in my memory like a film. I relive this memory from time to time. It is all mine to keep and treasure.

Some of the boys were wearing smart red shirts, others plain red T-shirts. The girls went all guns blazing, wearing beautiful red dresses. Vanuza looked so beautiful in a silky red dress with a large bow at the back and little red bows in her hair. The parents also tried and wore their Sunday best. We directed the parents to the chairs we had arranged in the main hall and led the children to their places, all sitting on the floor. We had prepared them well for their performance.

They were outstanding. They sang with us in their best voices. When they finished, each took a red rose to offer to their parents; at that moment time stopped, their daily struggle to do even the simplest of things disappeared, the constant dark cloud their parents lived under, wondering what will happen to their kids when they were gone, was momentarily forgotten. The only thing that existed in that moment was a pure exchange of love between the children and their parents.

The events of that day had a profound effect on me. I decided there and then that my destiny was in that field. I felt that much more could, and should, be done to improve these children's plights, to give them the best possible chance to achieve their potential and more importantly to lead better, more independent lives. I was about to finish senior school and was looking for a direction. Now I saw my path clearly lined up by the Milky Way. I felt invincible.

But what the Milky Way could not see, all the way down here on Earth, was that all the courses required to obtain the qualifications to work in that field were astronomically expensive. And to top that, most of the books were written in English.

I came crashing down to Earth at the speed of light.

I could not sleep at all that night; my internal dialogue was furiously trying to come up with possible solutions, only to encounter more obstacles.

I heard of a cheap English course at a school which had just opened; they were offering some good packages for working students, they also had a very flexible schedule that suited my hours. I thought at least I can start to learn English while I figure out how to finance my studies.

The school was basic. It occupied just half a floor in a very decrepit old building. As I could not speak a word of English, I could not tell if the teacher was any good. But the course was well structured, and I felt that at least that was a small step towards achieving my dream. Two weeks into the course, the owner of the school came into class with some exciting news.

'England is accepting au pair girls from South America in a two-year programme. The idea is that you go to England, live as an au pair with an English family performing light domestic duties, helping with the children a few hours a day. The rest of the day you are free to attend school and learn English.' He went on, 'You will receive £5 a week pocket money, your own room and food, all you need is to get your ticket. This is a golden opportunity, and I am now a partner with an agency in London who would easily place you. If you do well, you will be back in no time and if you manage to get the right certificates of English as a foreign language, I will employ you as one of my teachers.' He smiled broadly, all happy with himself for gate-crashing our lessons and being the bearer of good news.

'If any of you are interested come and see me after class.'

'I am, I don't need to see you after class, what do I have to do next?'

To this day, I don't really know what possessed me when I decided there and then that there was no other way out of my dilemma than flying 9,000 miles to England without speaking a word of English. I felt as if the position of the planets had just aligned, allowing my own butterfly effect to manifest itself in that classroom, in that tiny corner of São Paulo in the southern hemisphere of our tiny blue planet, propelling me to an unknown land to an even lesser-known destiny. In my sixteen-year-old mind, I would go, learn English, get the qualifications, come back, teach English, and finally be able to pay for my course and work with mentally challenged children in just a few years; my on going day dream of opening my own school, could perhaps become a reality one day.

Despite my epiphany, my impulsive decision and the logical internal dialogue that followed, mapping out my entire existence, I walked around in a daze, full of fear, not quite knowing what I was letting myself in for. There was a part of me that comforted my insecurities by telling myself that maybe no one would offer me a job anyway.

A letter was written on my behalf – my English was non-existent – and a response came after a few weeks with a full job offer to work for a young family in Edgware, North London. My duties were to look after two-year-old Jonathan and help with light household duties. I would go to school in the afternoons. The director of the school read the letter for me; the family was touched by the work I did at Don Patricio, and reassured me that England would broaden my horizons before I went back home to fulfil my dreams. He showed me pictures of a young couple and a beautiful blond boy with a chubby face and striking blue eyes. He looked like a cherub, all that was missing was his little harp.

I hadn't told a soul; deep down, it was too overwhelming for me to accept that I had been offered a position to work so far away from home in a different country. I was becoming my mother's daughter with secret schemes and dreams. I waited until the weekend to tell *Mamae*.

It was gnocchi Sunday at our house. Gnocchi Sundays were never-ending: they were long, lazy Sundays when I felt time had stood still after a long arduous week. Odecio

258

parked himself in a chair, reading the entire Sunday newspaper for hours on end, shaking his head, turning the pages back and forth indignant at the never-ending injustices committed by whoever was in power. All you could hear was him muttering obscenities under his breath and Iracy in the kitchen, buzzing like a little bee, singing her little tunes, totally concentrated on the messy and complicated process of making homemade gnocchi. Her day would start early: she would peel a ton of potatoes and while they cooked, she lined the kitchen table with flour. When the potatoes were soft, she would mash them with butter and a bit of milk and flour, mixing and kneading it until it turned into a dough. On that Sunday, I stayed by her side helping her. The dough would then be separated and rolled into long strips on the kitchen table; try as I might I could never get the dough to work for me and I would end up in an almighty mess. She would laugh at me and expertly take over, making precise strips of dough which were then cut into small squares before being thrown into a huge pot of salted boiling water where they floated to the top when cooked. I did not know how to state my situation and tell her of my plans. When everything was under control, with the gnocchi and her out-of-this-world homemade tomato sauce bubbling on the hob, I blurted out:

'*Mamae*, I want to go to England to learn English, come back, teach English, pay for my course, then go and work with the children.'

She continued to cut the little squares of dough and plop them into the boiling water. Looking at me intently for a long time, drinking in my agitation and uneasiness.

'The United States is very far, Kirinha, where did this idea come from? What is going on? You are not telling me the whole story.'

I told her the whole story from beginning to end.

'A job offer so far away? You are only a kid.'

'But you left to come here a lot younger.'

'The United States is far. How would I visit you?'

'It is England, *Mamae*, I will show you on the map, it is just a little further, in Europe.'

'I can see it in your face, and your altered breathing shows that this means a lot to you. I can see that there is no other escape route open to you.'

I showed her the letter and the photograph. She smiled.

'That's the whitest child I have ever seen and so beautiful, and the scribbles, is this English then? Is this what you will learn?'

'Yes, it is the future they say, it is an important language to learn.'

She turned around, put all the cooked gnocchi in a big glass dish and poured tomato sauce over it.

'Then you will go, I will find a way of getting you a ticket, leave it with me. Now call the others, the gnocchi is ready and don't breathe a word for now.'

I walked up to her. On gnocchi Sundays her apron, her clothes and even her hair ended up covered with flour and bits of tomato sauce. I hugged her. Words failed me.

She tried her hardest to get someone to sponsor me, even if it was just a bit towards my ticket. She knocked on government buildings, educational sectors of local council offices, colleges and universities. In the end she took out a loan for a one-way ticket to London Gatwick Airport. She had to find a guarantor as her credit was poor, so she knocked once again at Jojo's mother's door. Dona Lucineia was a loving, if tortured, soul, very Catholic and had no problem being a guarantor for my mother. Years later, I would discover that Iracy had no means of meeting the monthly payments and Dona Lucineia was left holding the bill. Decades later, I repaid her by giving her son a return plane ticket and enough pocket money to go back to Brazil to attend his father's funeral, although we were no longer together.

I shared the whole thing with Jojo.

'I know so much about England,' he said, 'I was going to go a few years back, but nothing came to fruition. I admire your courage.'

'Well, I will be back in no time at all, my destiny is to become a special needs teacher, even start my own school one day.'

'Maybe if I find a job and save enough money, I can meet you there later.'

'What would you do there?'

'I play the guitar, maybe I will join a rock band, be a rock star?'

I did not know what to do with that, so I left him to his dreams.

Now with a one-way ticket to London and a job offer there was no going back.

There was only one stumbling block. Odecio had to give his formal authorisation to allow me to obtain a passport as I was still a minor. Iracy had informed him of my dreams of going to England but avoided telling him how far ahead we both were with the preparations.

I heard the hushed tones of their disagreements concerning my imminent plans and my mother's total support and encouragement of them. Odecio could not bear the thought of allowing me to leave home so young to somewhere so far and inaccessible to him. He walked under a dark cloud. On the one hand he could see the logic and opportunities behind my plan but on the other he was full of fear for his only daughter.

The day came when he had to sign the papers authorising me to apply for a passport as a minor.

In a voice that struggled to come out of his throat, he said, 'This is absurd, it is all your mother's fault, I still don't approve of any of this. Promise me that you will learn as quickly as possible and return home. If anything happens to you go straight to the Brazilian Embassy, you will be safe and protected there.'

He quickly signed the papers, walked out of the door with a grim look on his face and left me standing there holding the signed forms.

Iracy was heavily criticised by her sisters. They could not fathom how she could allow me to jump on a plane and travel to a different continent so far away, all on my own.

'Anything could happen to her, there is no way to know if she is going to be ok or not. A letter will take ages to get here, Iracy! She is your only daughter, have you lost your mind?' protested Maria in a trembling voice, her eyes already welling up. Iracy understood more than anyone that my departure had deeply affected Maria who felt the loss of her own daughter every day until she took her last breath.

'She is your sweet girl, how can you let her go, Iracy?' cried Orminda.

'One more reason to let her go. She has no friends, she is far too sensitive, she cries far too much for my liking, she is always hanging around with us, listening to us, asking questions. She is drawn to our dramas. It is not natural, I don't think. She almost did not survive her first heartbreak.' She paused, 'And have you seen that lame duck hanging around her now? He is so much older, she tells me he listens to her, he understands her. Oh, good Lord.'

Iracy seemed to have the world on her shoulders. Her older sons were growing up fast with outside influences; they were beyond her control, always bringing home new ideas and new music that did not sit comfortably with Odecio. Their daily rows were making home life quite difficult. I have a feeling that she saw an opportunity to get her young daughter out of that environment. Years later when she came to visit me in England, she confessed that she knew I was never going to return.

She tried to make her sisters understand that she saw the determination in my eyes, the absolute trust I had in my master plan. She understood more than anyone else how important it was to have plans, to have impossible dreams. She could not ignore her daughter's insistence and deny her the opportunity to have a go at life.

São Paulo, 18th February 1975

After months of preparation, trepidation, and much internal hesitation on my part, the day of my departure to England finally came.

Odecio, my aunties and even important people who had visited England, came to give me advice on what to do, how to behave in England and what to say. They had all forgotten a minor detail; my English was non-existent.

No one in my entire family had set foot inside an airport, let alone an airplane.

In addition to my mother, father, brothers and Jojo, most of my aunties and uncles came with their children to see me off. It was an event not to be missed. It was as if I was the first Brazilian teenage girl to be launched into space.

They caused such a commotion at Congonhas Airport. They were loud, excited by the experience, they laughed, hugged me, gave me endless advice. Auntie Maria and Auntie Orminda held arms in a corner and talked in hushed tones with forlorn expressions. Odecio argued with my brother Cesar over some European political disagreement or another. Heathcliff and Wilson fooled around with our cousins.

I stood there next to *Mamae*, as if in a dream. We did not talk; we did not look at each other. There were no words left to say. She had accomplished the impossible for me and I was on my away. Panic started to engulf me. She noticed straight away and held my sweaty hands tight. I could feel her force, her energy and her courage as she squeezed my hand.

My flight was called, I left her and went to do the rounds of farewells. Odecio cried.

'If anything happens, if you don't like it there, head straight to the Brazilian Embassy; they will take care of you. Keep the address I gave you safe. If it goes well, promise me you will be back in a year, eighteen months maximum.'

'I promise, *Papai.*' That's all I could master.

Jojo promised to join me as soon as he could.

I hugged my aunties. *Tia* Orminda just shook her head in disbelief; *Tia* Maria would not look me in the eye.

'Go with God, Kirinha, pray the way I taught you.'

I hugged her, walking away as fast as I could. I knew only too well that Auntie Maria and I had the potential to flood the departure lounge with our tears.

Then the time to hug her, to thank her, to promise her that I would learn fast and be home in no time at all, was upon me. I felt as if I was having an extrasensory experience, I felt as if what I was about to do all on my own, leaving everyone and everything I knew behind, was not truly happening to me. She must have noticed my disorientation. She walked purposely towards me and held me in a strong embrace for a long time.

'This is what you wanted, this is what you dreamt of, and this is what you orchestrated for yourself, now hold your head up high like a grown-woman, turn your back, enter that plane and do not look back. Go!'

She stood there, like a statue, with a distant look on her face. That time not a single tuneful note came out of her mouth to comfort her. Maria and Orminda came to the rescue. They put their arms around her, turned her around and walked away with her. Deep down they knew that Iracy had given me the highest form of love; she set me free, she gave me wings to fly even if it was nine thousand long miles away from her.

I tried but I couldn't follow her instructions and I looked back; I saw my father, my brothers, Jojo, my uncles, my cousins. I waved and saw them waving back. My father waved with all his vigour encouraging me but the way he bit his lower lip betrayed his inner turmoil. I waved some more with my heart in pieces, finally realising that I wouldn't be seeing any of them the next day, or the day after, or anytime soon. I got on the plane and was surprised at how small it was inside, I collapsed into my seat and when the first tear broke free, the rest followed like a stream. I bent forward, put my head in my hands and start to cry with the force of a person spilling her guts for all to see.

All things must pass

Over four decades have passed since that day in February when my family caused a commotion at Congonhas Airport, São Paulo, whilst seeing me off.

My communication with my mother, father and brothers — for the first two decades at least — was conducted via letters. There was no phone at our house and the calls from England cost £1 per minute and my wages as an au pair were £5 per week, if I got paid.

When I stepped into the house in Edgware, North London where I was going to work as an au pair, Iracy's letters were already there waiting for me. She had written them while I was still in Brazil, by her side, getting ready for my long journey.

Kirinha,

I know when you read this letter you will be in England. I am writing it as you sleep and dream of a new life still under our roof, in our home in São Bernado dos Campos, where for the first time at the age of sixteen we could give you your own bedroom. A teenage bedroom that you will not get the chance to enjoy as you depart in search of a future. But I know that when you receive and open this letter you will be feeling confused, afraid and overwhelmed. I also know that you will have

268

red swollen eyes from crying. I also have a strong feeling that you will be feeling that you made a big mistake, wishing for a way to run back home.

I ask you not to panic. I encourage you to give this new situation, however tough and alien it may seem, at least a couple of months, maybe a little longer.

It has not been easy for me to let you go to such a strange and far away land, but it is a choice you made with unstoppable determination. I hope you can gain all the benefits you explained to me and learn English. This will open new horizons for you.

When you feel alone and far away from us here, think that I am right there by your side, every minute of every single day. An ocean cannot keep me away from you. My letters will be arriving to support you, to give you courage. Send news as soon as you can.

Papai and the boys are a bit quiet and the house feels empty without you. But life will go on, it always does. Please don't concern yourself with us back home and put all your energy into settling where you are.

Te amo

Mamae

Those first letters gave me the strength I lacked and the courage I needed to cope with my new life in England. It soothed the panic I felt when I arrived and my new reality dawned on me – I was in a strange country, among strangers speaking incomprehensible sounds to me, and 9,000 miles away from her.

Another manuscript or even a few more are needed if I am to tell all the events of the past forty-two years and all the stories still so vivid in my memory. Who knows what will happen to all these stories? Maybe I will continue to ask questions of those still living; maybe I will be writing for the rest of my days, such is the healing power of putting down on paper, to emotionally purge, the chaos and the wonder we call life. But for now, I will relate the vital times we crossed that vast ocean to be together in sadness and in joy. In all the decades, years, months, weeks, days that we were apart, I always felt her benevolent loving soul beside me.

Iracy's hunch, the feeling that I would never return to Brazil, did not lie. My dream of becoming a special needs teacher did not come true either. My life in England became a survival quest and survive I did, even thrived.

But she always taught me that when a dream is broken, dream another one or two – just keep on dreaming, planning and scheming. And I did just that, some new dreams did come true, and some didn't. I am still the eternal dreamer of infinite possibilities not just for myself but for all of us, for our entire human race.

I visited many times. I will never forget taking my second husband, Paul, to meet Iracy, Odecio, my brothers, aunties and cousins. Jojo did come to England, he did not become a rock star, we married and tried as much as we could, but we didn't work out; yet another story silently sleeping in the labyrinth of my psyche.

There was such a furore at Guarulhos International Airport as Paul, and I were welcomed by everyone. Words cannot describe what went on in my heart when we were all reunited once again. Time melted away, I felt as if I had never gone way. When we got to my parents' new house in Tucuruvi, São Paulo I spotted a large banner, written in English, across the front gate:

Welcome home Kirinha and Pull

She had gone to a lot of trouble to have that banner made in English. No one had the heart to point out to her the misspelling in Paul's name. We loved it. It was heavenly sitting in her kitchen, eating her food and *fuba* cake once again, with my brothers and father all loudly talking at the same time.

So much had happened in my parents' lives, in my brothers' lives, in my own life. So many stories still to be told. The letters crossing the transatlantic flight paths never stopped and we shared as much as we could but there was no substitute for catching up face to face. No photos of my nieces and nephews could replace the emotion of seeing them for the first time, drinking in their little faces, their hair colour, the light that shone from their eyes, their cries and their laughter as they stared at this stranger of an auntie trying her best to make them feel at ease, trying to make some sort of connection. However, love has the power to transcend space, time and the limits of human understanding. Despite the distance, I was fortunate that most of them were able to come and spend some time with me in England.

Just a year or so after meeting Paul, it was Iracy who would hop on an airplane for the first time in her life and endure a twelve-hour flight to come to my rescue. After a pregnancy riddled with scares, I gave birth to my first son, Daniel. He was very premature, and his lungs were not developed enough, so after attempting with all his strength to keep on breathing, his tiny lungs gave up on him and he died. A part of me died with him and as for the other parts, they were numb, disassociated from day-to-day living. During that heart-wrenching time, I thought a lot about my grandmother Francisca, *vovó* Chiquinha, and her many losses; every time a child died, she died a little more inside, leaving that familiar cavernous emptiness that slowly became a part of her. I wondered if it was possible to overcome that same cavernous emptiness I now felt in my own being.

Iracy arrived all by herself, without speaking a word of English, at Heathrow Airport. She somehow managed to navigate her way through immigration, luggage collection and customs. The sight of my tiny *mamae*, pushing her trolley with a case full of rice, beans, maize for the *fuba* cake and gifts for Paul and me from all the family, kick-started my heart with a high voltage of hope. She was sixty-two years old and I was thirty-two. She was unwell, her blood pressure was extremely high at night and too low in the morning. She had these awful ulcers all over her legs. She had travelled against the doctor's orders to come to me. Wilson facilitated this for both of us, got her the ticket and put her on the plane. I don't think he has any idea of the enormity of the gift he gave us.

During the months she stayed with me, I had the golden opportunity to relate to my mother as an adult woman. I, inspired by her single-minded sense of purpose, had managed to build my own life in England. I was now living in Bournemouth and making a career at an American bank. Many years back, after leaving my CV with all the Brazilian firms in London asking for a job, my lucky break came when Banco Real called me to help them out temporarily and there, I stayed for seven years, learning some vital banking skills. Once again, Banco Real shone a light in the darkness for me.

Mamae and I went everywhere sightseeing in Bournemouth, Dorset and London. She enjoyed every day with that zest for life and sense of wonder that was so typically hers. I took her to the doctors, who reduced her medication, and suggested a healthy diet and long walks. Soon, her blood pressure was under control and the ulcers on her legs were cleared by a prescribed cream – she even took a pot of this cream to her sister, Maria. And as for my broken heart: she showed me how to heal.

'Kirinha, I hope the loss of your baby son will not destroy you. That would be heart-breaking for me to see you give up on yourself, your husband and this lovely life you struggled to build for yourself. Yes, cry your tears, be bereaved, but go outside, smell the sea air, look around you. Please give life another chance. You will have a girl and a boy before your 40th birthday and don't let anyone tell you that you left it too late and whatever nonsense they may throw at you.'

She was right, I was to be blessed with a girl and a boy. By the time I was 38, two brand new lives burst into mine; tiny mouths gasping for air taking their first breath, little lungs inflating, beginning to work on their own, moving oxygen into mixed Tupi Guarani, African and Anglo-Saxon blood; hungry mouths already searching for their sustenance, already fighting for survival; they filled me with blissful adoration, an elated state of joy; they opened my awareness to such pure love that made everything that had gone before worth it, helping to heal the ancestral trauma stored in my DNA; in the midst of my rough earthliness, seeing even the most ordinary of things through their full-of-wonder eyes, made life became brand new again.

During the months we spent together in England, she lost weight, tried to learn to swim and embraced healthy eating. She returned a changed woman and very stunning indeed at the age of sixty-two, a lot slimmer, wearing new clothes and even stylish sunglasses. Upon her return she joined a local club in Tucuruvi and enjoyed looking after herself a bit more. Her visit changed both of us.

After her visit to England, I continued to visit Brazil; she also came to England with Odecio a couple of times to meet their Anglo-Brazilian grandchildren. These joyful occasions are imprinted in my brain; they warm my heart to this day. Odecio and Iracy caused a riot everywhere they went, Odecio's attempts at speaking English with the natives and the confusion it caused, left me in stitches. They found a reason to laugh at everything and everyone, including Paul. They spoilt the children and broke some of our parental rules behind our backs.

They cause a commotion at Boots trying to buy a dummy for baby Bianca against my orders by using all their creativity and gestures to make themselves understood with the shop assistants and some customers that gathered around them until a dummy was found.

'Chupeta!!' they both shouted at the same time.

'Chupeta – Dummy,' the shop assistants repeated back, laughing and totally relieved to give them what they wanted and get rid of them.

They were like a couple of unruly naughty children.

Then one day, the secret fear that I carried with me throughout my life in England, living so far away from them, came to haunt me.

I received the news that Odecio was dying. I jumped on the first available plane to São Paulo. I managed to catch him still alive. He smiled at me.

'You got here fast, Kirinha,' he said, struggling for breath.

'Yes, I was lucky to get a flight and I am here now, and I have brought you some gifts and magazines and articles about the Second World War.' Odecio was an expert on WW2, he read intensely on the matter and was always eager to get new material: I went on and on, dozens of words rushing out of me, desperately trying to keep him engaged, awake, alive.

'You came, you managed to get here, and well, thank you. We can look at them when I get out of here, you look so beautiful. Where is your brother? He went to fetch my dentures; I must have them on.'

Francoise La Dulce found the dentures, put them in for him, combed his hair.

'There Uncle, you look beautiful, try and relax now.' He looked at her tenderly, closed his eyes; his heart was giving up on him fast.

He was hospitalised at A&E in one of São Paulo's public hospitals. The visits were restricted to two relatives at a time, so a small army of family and friends gathered in the hospital foyer waiting for their turn. With the help of my cousin and childhood partner in crime, Eliete, who had trained as a midwife and ran a medical centre in one of São Paulo's periphery areas, I was able to spend more time with him, disguised as a health professional complete with overall and a badge. After a few days, the doctor in charge of the emergency unit gathered my mother, brothers and I to give us an update.

'There is no easy way of sharing this with you as I am not just talking about one of the patients here but your husband, Dona Iracy and of course the father of your children here. Senhor Odecio's clinical profile is not promising. He is very weak, and his chances of survival are indeed almost non-existent.'

We stood there looking at the floor and gathering the courage to look at Odecio, drifting in and out of consciousness. My father who had been such a big presence in my life, so full of life, so humanly real, now lay there in a hospital bed, his skin grey, his body so frail and small like a child.

I looked at the doctor in charge of all that human misery and I noticed how young she was. I noticed her trainers and jeans underneath her white overalls. I noticed the dark circles under her eyes: dark rings of purple and grey in a young face. I sensed how exhausted she was. I felt great respect for this young woman. She was doing her very best, working in appalling conditions with very limited resources, and yet she had taken the time to clarify things for us and even go beyond the call of duty, carefully choosing her words to soften the blow.

A day later, when I was by his bedside with Auntie Maria, his breathing became irregular and the machine he was attached to, which aided his breathing, started bleeping quite loudly. There was a commotion of nurses and doctors who rushed to his side. They put electrodes stuck to large sticky pads on his chest. The electrodes were connected to a defibrillator machine, and he was given several controlled electric shocks to his chest. Auntie Maria and I held on to each other tightly as we watched Odecio take his final breath. We nearly drowned in each other's tears.

Iracy was home. Unknown to everyone, when he was first hospitalised, she had to make one of the toughest decisions of her life. The doctors explained to her that to save his life, they would have to amputate both of his legs.

'And can you tell me, how many years is he likely to live after the amputation?'

'It is an important question but a difficult one to answer. There are many factors involved, including the mental impact this will have on your husband, he could last another six months or even a few more years.'

'Where do I sign to give you the authority NOT to amputate his legs and allow nature to take its course.'

She was certain he was going to die on that day. She had stayed at home preparing one of his favourite navy-blue suits, a pristine white shirt and a blue tie. She gave his best pair of black leather shoes the perfect shine. She knew her husband well.

She sent Heathcliff to the hospital.

'It is time my son, go to your father, take his suit and shoes with you, tell them to dress him with care.'

Odecio's funeral was attended by dozens of relatives and friends. He looked dashingly handsome in his open coffin. So many people I had never met came to console me, sharing stories of his many acts of kindness towards them and their families.

Iracy did not shed a single tear. However, her inability to cry would manifest itself in different ways. She would wake up with her body covered in bruises, the inside and outside of her mouth covered in ugly cold sores. Sometimes she would stay in bed for days with what she called kidney pains. No medical explanation was ever found for her kidney pains.

As I write I am sitting on a little veranda overlooking the Himalayas in Dharamshala, India. I am on a yoga and meditation retreat. Yoga and meditation have been my dear companions for many years and have helped me to find my centre, my equilibrium. I am also here for some solitude, to connect with my inner creator and to put the finishing touches to *The Mother of Honey*.

This under-developed part of India is breathtakingly beautiful. It reminds me of Minas Gerais and all the holidays we spent with Iracy visiting our relatives, in the heart of rural Brazil in the 1960s. I feel very close to *Mamae*; it is a surreal feeling, as if a part of her is here with me.

I have been very fortunate as the Dalai Lama is here during my stay and I am attending four days of his teachings.

At the outset of the 1959 Tibetan uprising, fearing for his life, the Dalai Lama and his retinue fled Tibet, crossing to India in March 1959. He eventually set up the Government of Tibet in Exile in Dharamshala, in a small town called Mcleod Ganj. He created a Tibetan educational system to teach the Tibetan children their language, history, religion and culture. Many Tibetan refugees are established here now; I feel as if I am in Tibet as I walk around the temple among Tibetan citizens and monks.

I am sitting next to a Tibetan lady; she is the spitting image of *Mamae*. She even keeps feeding me cake – sadly not *fuba* cake – and is patiently teaching me to sing the mantra 'Om Mani Padme Hum' – Tibetan Buddhists believe that saying the mantra out loud, or silently to oneself, invokes the powerful benevolent attention and blessings of Chenrezig, the embodiment of compassion.

I feel at peace; my heart, which has been so heavy since she had to be put in a home, feels lighter at the Dalai Lama temple, eating moon cake, drinking the butter tea served by the monks and singing this mantra with my new Tibetan friend and everyone around me.

The Dalai Lama shares many of his beliefs on compassion to all sentient beings, and unity among all races and religions. He talks of the imminent need for a global education system that inspires children to cultivate benevolence towards others and their communities, changing young minds from an individualistic, materialistic viewpoint to developing a more compassionate heart. An educational system that would free young minds to find creative solutions to save the planet – not just for the domination of a few but for all living beings. As I listen to the Dalai Lama, sitting on the floor next to my new Tibetan friend, that surreal feeling of Iracy's benevolent, loving presence engulfs me once again. I feel happy; I have been checking in with Wilson via WhatsApp.

1st October 2017

Hi Wilson, I climbed the first part of the Himalayas, a trek called Triund, it is very popular with the locals. I left at 6 am and came back at 4 pm. It was difficult but climbing down was worse, it rained a lot, and the stony path became dangerously slippery but what scared the hell out of me were the little donkeys trailing up and down the mountain, loaded with goods. How are you? How is Mamae*? Xxxx*

Hi Kira, how cool, I am glad you are enjoying your trip. I thought you were already back, have you decided to move to India? Everything is fine here, Mamae *is the same. I will ask for some tests next week; from time to time she has urine infections.*

Wilson, I came to stay a month doing yoga, meditation and lots of walking. It is my 60th birthday present to myself ☐ Poor Mamae*, these urine infections are treacherous for the elderly. ☹*

6th October 2017

Hi Kira, how are you? Listen, I am taking Mamae *to A&E; she hasn't been eating at all well for days; she is so weak, appears to be dehydrated. I called Heathcliff and Cesar to come with me. Will keep you informed. xxxxxxxxxx*

Thank you, Wilson. Please keep me informed and if it is necessary, I will leave India and go directly to São Paulo. How is she mentally? Xxxxxxx

Mentally she is well, but she simply answers what is asked of her, sometimes, she gets a little confused, but she recognises everyone and remembers things. She has hardly eaten anything; she is refusing food, I think this is what is debilitating her; the doctor will ask for blood and urine tests, perhaps some x-rays. Let's keep chatting here. Xxxxxxxx

Please do. xxxxx

Heathcliff just arrived; Cesar is on his way. xxxxx
Excellent. What do you think if Mamae and I face-timed? Xxxx

She will not be able to focus or see you, she will be very confused. xxx

OK. ☹

She has been put on a drip. We don't yet know if she will stay hospitalised or whether she will be sent back to the nursing home, will keep you informed. xxxx

Kira, she may be transferred to another hospital, the one you stayed at with her about two years ago, before she had to go into a home. Xxx

Ok Wilson, I feel that hospital is more equipped to run some proper tests. xxx

On that very same night, I try to get a flight from Dharamshala to São Paulo. There are no direct flights; it will take me two or three days to get there. I call Paul and ask him to book me on the first flight back to London; it will be easier to fly from London if she gets worse.

7th October 2017

Kira, she has been transferred to the hospital in Mooca. I think her recuperation will be faster there than if she returns to the nursing home. Cesar is staying with her. Let's keep talking here. xxxx

Agree Wilson, she is better off there. Paul is booking my flights to London. I am cutting my retreat short. Today I have a day sightseeing. Please WhatsApp me, I will be picking up my messages during the day xxxxx

Go Kira, do your sightseeing in peace. I will not disturb you unless it is something serious xxx

*No, you are not disturbing me at all,
keep me informed xxx It is already Saturday
here.*

That Saturday, I take a cab and spend
the day going through various churches and
Buddhists temples, a Tibetan cultural centre
and some historical sights. Although I do not
follow any religion, I love the quietude and the
still calmness of an empty church or temple.
The first stop is an ancient Christian church,
very small inside. I sit there, being engulfed
once again by her benevolent loving presence.
I have an internal dialogue with her.

'Hi, *Mame*, my warrior. I hope that
whatever happens, you don't suffer any
discomfort or pain, I hope that you feel
peaceful. I want you to get well, I want to throw
another big party for your 91st birthday just like
the one we threw in April with all of us, and
with Gilberto, Carlos – those boys you
mothered for a while – their children, their
grandchildren all around you.' I say a little
prayer, asking for the best outcome for her.

8th October 2017
*Wilson, how is she? Has she perked up
a bit? And the infection, is she more hydrated?
Xxxxxx*

*Kira, just arrived at the hospital,
Heathcliff is here. She refuses to eat. She is*

*very weak. I hope she can fight this infection.
xxxx*

Wilson, how are you coping? xxxx

I am well. I feel these situations can occur at any time. I am leaving the responsibility of staying with her 24/7 with Heathcliff and Cesar; I think it is for the best that they do this for her right now. Xxxxx

Wilson, I think so too. It is healthier for you not to take all this responsibility alone. I am booking my flight to London as it is proving difficult to fly to São Paulo from here. xxxxx

It is your decision, Kira, your presence here is always very welcome xxx
9th October 2017
Kira, she is very weak. The doctor is putting her on another drip – through her nose – to pump some nutrients into her body. She may have to return to the nursing home, like this. xxx

Wilson, this approach may help her gain some strength. It seems to me she is back where she was two and half years ago, however, last time her fighting spirit to get better was still present. I feel she is tired of fighting … maybe she has had enough ☹ Paul has booked my flights; I leave here tomorrow and get to London on Thursday morning. Xxxxx

Kira, our mother's hands and arms are very swollen. According to the nurse, it could be water retention – a kidney problem. She will be assessed to establish a course of treatment. She sleeps all the time. I don't feel very optimistic, minha irma. *It is sad but I can't see a way out of this. Xxxxxx*

☹ ☹ *Wilson, I also feel the time for her to leave us is fast approaching. I arrive in London on Thursday. Paul is already looking for flights to São Paulo.* ☹ ☹

10th October 2017

I get up at 5 am. I slept an agitated sleep. I stayed up late putting the finishing touches to *The Mother of Honey*. I had a sudden flow of creative energy all this week, entire sentences, scenes flooding my mind, all the while engulfed by that surreal feeling of her benevolent loving presence. Outside of my room, there is a little veranda, overlooking the Himalayas. I sit there in the darkness, meditating, when a hazy green and pink light appears out of nowhere, entering my room, I follow it, it shines on my bed, I lie on top of the blankets allowing the light to penetrate every cell of my body, every speck of awareness in my consciousness. I know it is her. I don't know how long I stay there but when I open my eyes, the sun has risen. I get up, get ready, leave the yoga centre and take a long walk through the mountains to the Dalai Lama temple. I breathe the cool morning air, taking in the beauty of my surroundings, hearing the birdsong as if in a dream. A few hours later, I go back to my room, switch my phone back on. I have several missed calls from Wilson and from Paul and a WhatsApp from Wilson.

My sister, our beloved mother has left us just a few minutes ago. She did not suffer; she was not in pain. Our warrior is gone.

No one warned me about the unbearable physical pain I would feel from losing my mother. I feel as if my belly button has been cut open and my connection to her brutally amputated. I am in unfathomable pain howling like an animal, crouched on the floor, rocking myself back and forth. The pain she felt with me entering the world, I feel with her leaving it.
I feel alone, with no shelter, no map, no compass.

8th November 2017 São Bernardo dos Campos, São Paulo – Bournemouth, England via FaceTime.

Twenty-nine days have passed since her death. There were dozens of people at her funeral paying their respects. She looked

288

beautiful in her coffin, her indigenous dark skin glowed once again and that beautiful face I love so much, looked peaceful.

. With Bianca by my side, I gathered the courage to go to the Teodoro Campos Sao Paulo clinic. I had a gift for an angel who lived there.

I found Dona Rita sitting on her bed, as usual in front of her Zimmer frame. The look of slight panic on her face frightened me: was I doing the right thing, come here to tell her of my mother's death?

'Where is she? where is Iracy? don't tell me, I knew it, I have been asking the helpers, asking the Manager, but they wouldn't't tell me, they don't let us know. But I knew, I knew.'

'I had to come and see you and tell you Dona Rita, I am sorry if it is against the procedure here. I bought you a gift from London'.

She gave me a sad smile. 'No, you have done the right thing, I am so glad to see you and who is this beauty here? Bianca, right?'

Bianca walked over and kissed her.

I shared with her that my mother went peacefully, with no discomfort or pain and when one of the nurses asked her how she was when she was first hospitalised, she simply said, 'I feel very well, I am well, and how are you?'

Dona Rita went on to share with Bianca and I her many losses and that she was glad that Iracy had finally rested.

'She was a tough cookie your mum, she made me laugh, but recently she had been so quiet, she was fading yes, fading…. but every morning as I walked past her room, I saw her hand outstretched calling me over. I would walk over to her bed, and she would hold my hand and kiss it, and I would kiss her – good morning Iracy, did you sleep well?'

'Yes, I slept with the angels and the devil, *minha amigona* – my great friend – then she would laugh.'

Dona Rita insisted on accompanying us to the front door, slowly moving her Zimmer frame in front of her. We kept waving and blowing kisses for a long time until the front gates had to be finally shut on us.

Today, my brothers will be spreading her ashes at a nature spot in São Bernardo dos Campos. I am back in England, and they will FaceTime me. It was in that part of Greater São Paulo that, against all odds, she bought her first house, saving us from homelessness, with her usual determination, fierce intuition and that unfathomable force that existed in her. It was in that house during a gnocchi Sunday that I shared with her my dream of coming to England.

The physical pain I felt when she died is subsiding with each passing day as I focus on my healing. I have gone back to work. My deferred dream of being in a helping profession has finally come true but not in the way I had so precisely planned all those decades ago. I am now a psychotherapist. My job is to try to alleviate people's hearts when it all gets too much to bear. I am also doing rewarding work with a mentally challenged boy who has been referred to me by his father.

It is time to spread her ashes and let her fly. It is 2 pm here in Bournemouth, via face time, I can see Cesar, Heathcliff, Wilson and Luiz Henrique, our childhood and long-life friend that lived next door to us at Rua Assungui.

Cesar is spreading her ashes into this beautiful lake; he decides to keep a bit of her ashes with him. Heathcliff watches quietly. His heart is filled with both sadness and joy; a couple of years ago, in his early sixties, he finally found love, tied the knot with a sweet woman who is now pregnant; Heathcliff will become a father in May next year. Luiz Henrique's presence and his strong spiritual beliefs in Candomblé – an African-American religious tradition practiced mainly in Brazil – ensure Iracy is well accompanied as she leaves the material plane. We all listen to Wilson as he reads some words I put together; they came to me out of the blue while that surreal feeling of her benevolent loving presence engulfed me once again.

Yes, miss me, but not too much

I don't want to see you forlorn and taciturn.

I want to see you happy, living your lives – just like I lived mine, with a joyful soul.

Believe that the strength of my spirit, the love and hope I have always had for the four of you will live forever within your hearts.

And when you see a sun rise, the first flowers of spring, a sky full of stars, the smiles on the lips of your children and grandchildren, or when you laugh your scandalous delicious laugh, you can be certain that I still exist in all those things, I live in all that is beautiful around you

Now let me go, be at peace, let me fly above the forests, the rivers, the waterfalls, let me play on the arches of rainbows, let me leap from star to star

And please remember what I always told you kids, life is a borrowed gift and must go on. Live it with purpose, live it with gusto!

Yes, miss me, but not too much … let me go.

Fuba Cake

Ingredients (8 servings)
• 1 cup (tea) of margarine
• 1 cup (tea) of sugar
• 4 egg yolks
• 1 cup (tea) of wheat flour
• 1/2 cup (tea) cornstarch
• 1 cup (tea) of cornmeal
• 1 tablespoon of baking powder
• 1/2 cup (tea) of orange juice
• 1 teaspoon of Fennel
• 4 egg whites, beaten into stiff peaks
To grease and flour
• Margarine
• wheat flour
Method of preparation
Grease and flour a pan with a central hole (22 cm in diameter). Reserve.

Preheat the oven to medium temperature (180° C).

Beat the margarine, sugar and egg yolks in a mixer for 3 minutes or until you get a fluffy, whitish cream.

Add the flour, cornstarch, cornmeal, yeast, fennel alternating with the juice. Mix without beating.

Add the egg whites, mixing gently.

Place the dough in the pan and bake for 40 minutes or until a toothpick inserted comes out clean. Let it cool.

Serve immediately with a fresh cup of coffee and lots of love.

Gratitude Corner

To my mother and father for believing in me, for their immense sacrifice to ensure my survival, for all the love they gave.

To my lovely aunts for keeping an open door for me and for all their prayers.

To my Paul, my Bianca, my Jack for everything. You gave me the gift of living with purpose and with great joy.

To my brothers for the childhood stories we share. The stories are ours to keep for ever.

To my nephews and nieces for the love and joy they always gave me.

My cousins for being my first best friends.

Last but not least, my soul sisters, Gilda, Joana, Peppa, Victoria. The Friday Frolics – Genoveva, Jean, Lorraine and Polly. I will be forever grateful for the way you opened your hearts to the writer in me. What would I do without you?

Infinite gratitude to the readers.

Printed in Poland
by Amazon Fulfillment
Poland Sp. z o.o., Wrocław